A SOLDIER'S WIFE

ALSO BY BLAIR UNDERWOOD

Before I Got Here: The Wondrous Things We Hear When We Listen to the Souls of Our Children

Casanegra (coauthor)

In the Night of the Heat (coauthor)

From Cape Town with Love (coauthor)

South by Southeast (coauthor)

Olympic Pride, American Prejudice (coauthor)

A SOLDIER'S WIFE

My Mother, the Marvelous Mrs. Marilyn A. Underwood

BLAIR UNDERWOOD
with Ylonda Gault

AMISTAD
An Imprint of HarperCollinsPublishers

All photos in this book are courtesy of the author.

Without limiting the exclusive rights of any author, contributor or the publisher of this publication, any unauthorized use of this publication to train generative artificial intelligence (AI) technologies is expressly prohibited. HarperCollins also exercise their rights under Article 4(3) of the Digital Single Market Directive 2019/790 and expressly reserve this publication from the text and data mining exception.

A SOLDIER'S WIFE. Copyright © 2026 by Blair Underwood. All rights reserved. No part of this book may be used or reproduced in any manner whatsoever without written permission except in the case of brief quotations embodied in critical articles and reviews. For information, address HarperCollins Publishers, 195 Broadway, New York, NY 10007. In Europe, HarperCollins Publishers, Macken House, 39/40 Mayor Street Upper, Dublin 1, D01 C9W8, Ireland.

HarperCollins books may be purchased for educational, business, or sales promotional use. For information, please email the Special Markets Department at SPsales@harpercollins.com.

hc.com

FIRST EDITION

Library of Congress Cataloging-in-Publication Data has been applied for.

ISBN 978-0-06-321187-2

Art on pages ii, iii, x, xix, xx, 15, 16, 43, 44, 63, 64, 75, 76, 97, 98, 111, 112, 139, 140, 157, 158, 171, 172, 175 © Shelley/stock.adobe.com

Designed by Michele Cameron

Printed in the United States of America

26 27 28 29 30 LBC 5 4 3 2 1

*I dedicate this book to my mother,
Marilyn Ann Underwood, who began weaving this book half a century ago and whose spirit has guided me to complete it with love, gratitude, and reverence. This work is yours, Mom. May it reflect your life's work that you so unselfishly poured into me: "Good measure, pressed down, shaken together and running over." I am overflowing with your love and in every beat of my heart, you live on because it was you . . .
who gave me life.*

*"Her children rise up and call her blessed;
her husband also, and he praises her."*
Proverbs 31:28

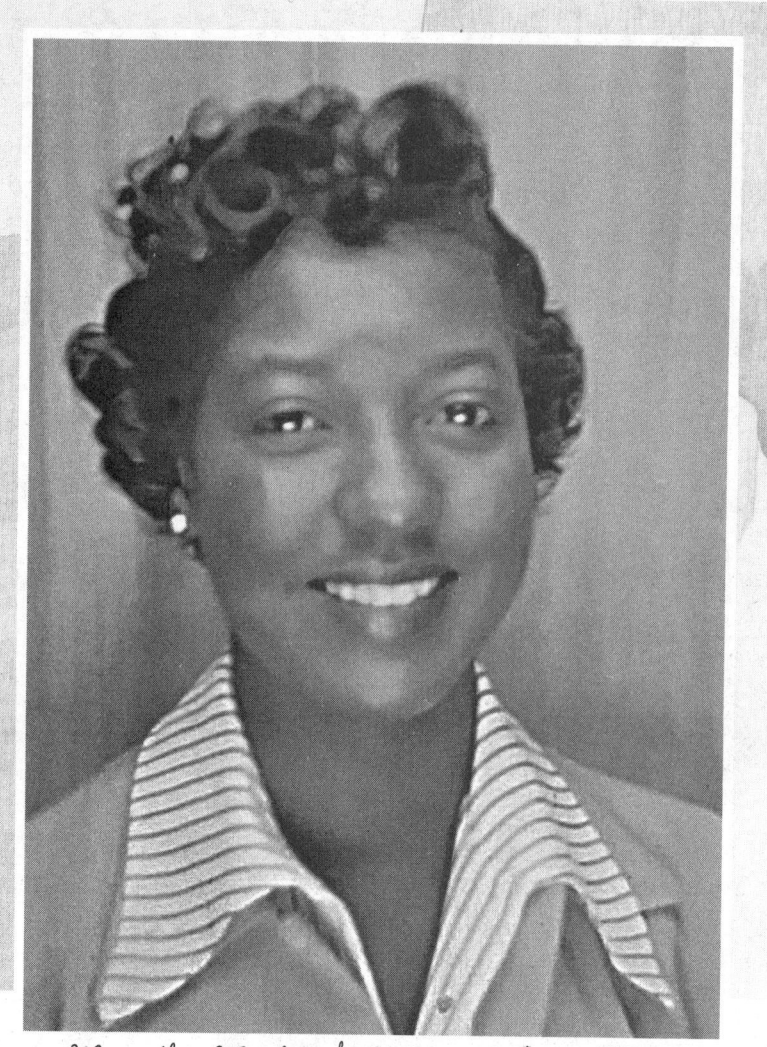

My mother, Marilyn A. Underwood. Circa 1954.

CONTENTS

Preface	xi
1 Wisdom	1
2 Devotion	17
3 Discipline	45
4 Perseverance	65
5 Letting Go	77
6 Success	99
7 Leadership	113
8 Faith	141
9 Duty	159
Afterword	173
Acknowledgments	177
About the Author	183

Our family in a photo in Colorado Springs, Colorado, 1973. From left to right: me, with my sister Marlo; our mom, Marilyn, and on her lap our family dog; our dad, Frank Sr.; and my brother, Frank Jr.

PREFACE

Quietly, steadfastly, and for many, many years, Mom had been putting together a memoir of sorts. She wasn't a professional writer. And I'm not sure whether she had been guided by a method or specific narrative style. But over the years she wrote frequently. None of us knew of the detail and dedication she put into what—on some level—we believed may have been a passing fancy. Mom had many ambitions. She was never afraid to dream and dream big. For instance, she always talked about completing a bachelor's degree. There were always travel plans, dinner party plans, and holiday plans. So many events, places, experiences she looked forward to going to and seeing.

While her physical body had left us on October 28, 2020, her spirit was very much with us, particularly in her writings and musings. The way she looked to the future, with optimism and change-the-world energy, was part of her infectious charm. Life was never stagnant with Mom—not in her advanced age and not even in the advanced stages of MS. To her, something great and exciting was always around the corner.

Throughout the years she would be scribbling in a notebook, writing down events and her thoughts around important life lessons—then I suppose life would step in and distract her from completing her vision. Periodically, she would announce to the family that she'd come up with a new title for The Book. I believe the last title may have been something like *Life from Four Feet High*. This was, of course, a nod to her perspective of the world from the wheelchair she'd been confined to for the past two decades.

Even with all her talk about her memoirs, when she passed at eighty-four, I was surprised to find so much evidence of the groundwork she'd been laying for such a project for so long. Even my siblings who'd become her primary caregivers, notably my sister Marlo—who served as her default stenographer—were struck by the volume of papers and materials she left behind.

To have a mom document her experiences from the routine to the remarkable is a gift, and one I wanted to share with the world, especially to fill in the blanks of unseen women like my mother who held families and communities together for generations.

I first envisioned this project as a children's book expressing the awe that I remembered as a child when we moved from one military base to another and my mother's efficient and effortless plans to not interrupt our routines, and to make wherever we lived feel like a home.

I suggested the idea to Judith Curr, my former publisher, and over a meal she told me that she saw something much larger than a children's book. A children's book would limit my mother to my perspective of her only as a mother, but she had lived a full adult life before merging her individual self with her identities as a wife and a mother. How could I bring all three of these personas in full context while also honoring her legacy and authenticity? Ideas began to percolate. I knew the title of the book had to be *A Soldier's Wife*. That's how I and so many people knew her—and the incomparable partnership she shared with my dad, Colonel Frank Underwood. She proudly accepted—even relished—that role. And on a sentimental note, one of the last performances my mother saw me in on Broadway was in a 2020 revival of Charles Fuller's 1982 Pulitzer Prize–winning play, *A Soldier's Play*. In an extraordinary company helmed by director Kenny Leon, I played Captain Richard Davenport—who the late, great Howard E. Rollins Jr. brought to the screen in the film adaptation. I still remember my mother, beaming with pride, at all my performances, and I received a Tony nomination for Best Leading Actor in a Play. Of course, COVID brought the show to an early close, but the memories still linger, especially of Mom's pride. Around the same time Mom had found joy in the streaming series *The Marvelous Mrs. Maisel*, about a New York housewife in the late 1950s who pursues a career as a stand-up comedian. Mom was such a fan of the series, in fact, that, at the Broadway premiere of *A Soldier's Play*, when she spotted actor Tony Shalhoub—who stars as the main character's dad—she nearly lost it.

The series was in some ways a stark contrast to Mom's life; I'm sure what drew her was the glamour of that period in Manhattan—a city she loved. But she also likely identified with Mrs. Maisel's moxie and creative ambition, since Mom, too, nursed artistic aspirations. As a tribute to who Mom had always been, I wanted to include *Marvelous* in the subtitle because that was an apt description of Mom.

I was at home in Los Angeles when my siblings lovingly called and put me on speakerphone so that I could be "with" her as she transitioned at home in Petersburg, Virginia. My dad, siblings, and I said our goodbyes. After decades of pain and suffering from multiple sclerosis, her passing was not entirely unexpected. But that doesn't mean we were ready. How do you prepare yourself for the physical loss of the most important woman in your life?

* * *

PREFACE

MS, I've learned, is a very complicated autoimmune disease. There's no cure. And researchers don't know the cause—possibly it's linked to your environment, maybe genetics? It's not a terminal illness, the average lifespan is twenty-five to thirty-five years after diagnosis. Although a person doesn't exactly die from MS, the complications—like chronic urinary tract infections, and challenges with swallowing and breathing—often lead to death. I didn't know it at the time, but in the weeks leading up to her death Mom had stopped eating. She was weak and very thin. Her spirits, as always, were high. She never let on how much she was suffering.

The pandemic had, of course, made each aspect of everyday life more challenging, but my family managed to have an exquisite homegoing service. Mom's grandchildren spoke. My three siblings—Frank Jr., Marlo, Mellisa—and I shared remembrances. It was truly joyful and uplifting. Just as Mom was.

In the weeks that followed, her words "I need to tell my story" echoed like a mission. Not in an ego-centered way—Marilyn Ann Scales Underwood prided her role as a humble servant for all of her years. So, her motivation for sharing her story was completely selfless. She knew her life—a powerful testimony of love, creativity, dedication, and God's grace—could help somebody, and probably lots of *somebodies*.

The idea of service defined my mom, really. It was

the core of her being. She lived in service to her husband—my dad, Colonel Frank Underwood—a veteran serviceman himself in the US Army. In service to her children, her community. And above all, in service to her Lord and Savior, Jesus Christ.

And, as God would have it, when we went through her memorabilia we began finding notes Mom had been writing; ideas she'd dictated, when she could no longer write on her own; and all kinds of treasured notes, articles, and letters she'd held on to. It wasn't amazing that she kept things—Mom was a "saver," never threw out anything. There were mounds of notebooks and papers by her bedside at all times. It's been a blessing to look back on her life in her own words. In that way, among countless others, Mom has remained very close to us.

Of course, all of us have stories—rich, stirring, and funny accounts of Mom being her iconic self. Dad can go on for hours about Mom's intelligence, beauty, loyalty, and personality—how blessed he was to have the perfect service wife in the military and in civilian life. Mellisa cracks us up about the time Dad called the house once while Mom was napping. And as Mellisa handed her the receiver, Mom made Mellisa bring her earrings to the bedside—so she could look and feel her best, even just to have a phone conversation with her husband.

Marlo has shared some of the times she looks back on from the day or so prior to Mom's passing. Her body

PREFACE

was weak and frail, and her energy understandably low. Still she woke up with a mission and insisted that Marlo help her get herself together so she could cast her vote in the pivotal 2020 presidential election.

Frank Jr. remembers funny conversations he and Mom shared about the kind of woman he should consider for marriage and those he should avoid. Mama kept it real.

We can laugh and enjoy her bigger-than-life personality. And it dawned on me that, after all she gave us, we can now give to her. We can help fulfill one of her longtime dreams—the same way she always worked to fulfill ours. My family and I painstakingly combed through Mom's stacked collection of jottings on scratch paper, in notebooks and journals. We combed through old text messages; listened to cassette tapes and voicemail recordings; and we pored over family videos, on VHS no less, from back in the day. Don't even get me started on the photographs we found.

What I knew but never fully processed is that with every move—from one army base to another—Mom never threw out *anything*. Up in the attic of the house we moved to just before my dad retired—I was around fourteen or fifteen at the time—were boxes and boxes of baby announcements, report cards, graduation or class assembly programs, family albums, journals. You name it. They were all like pieces of fabric woven into the tapestry of Mom's life.

PREFACE

In many ways, once my siblings and I realized how much material we had, this book practically wrote itself. We knew it was important to tell my mother's story in the way she would've wanted to tell it if she were still here—not through our eyes, but from her point of view. After all, everything she did throughout her life was in service to us. She took great pride in being a wife and mother. The voice throughout these pages is an amalgam of her writings. To be clear this isn't a memoir but more of a remembrance of a life lived well. While dates and times are significant, this isn't a book written in chronological order but instead as an expression of Mom's core values. And these virtues are not the totality of who she was as a woman, as a creative, as a child of God. Each chapter you will read here was chosen to represent the tenets Mom embraced and lived most fiercely. Wisdom. Faith. Family. Courage. Duty. Perseverance. These are the principles and stories that defined her.

*Like these pearls I put on every day.
And I do mean Every. Single. Day.
Each one a symbol—of wisdom, devotion,
discipline, perseverance, letting go, success,
leadership, and faith. It's part of who I am;
it's who we all are.*

Taking Mom for a stroll around the neighborhood, Petersburg, Virginia, Sept 2018, while filming When They See Us in New York.

1

WISDOM

Hold on now. See, some days the clasp acts up. Or maybe it's my grip. No, it's the clasp. These pearls and I have been through a lot together—good days as well as those that maybe fell short of good days. Each morning. First thing. The way some people reach for their glasses, I put on my pearls. They're pretty, but not just pretty. Necessary.

Nothing is easy in this life. But I'm here. And it's only right to be the best me I can be every day. MS is a disease that comes like a thief in the night. To rob your body and your spirit. I don't like it one bit. And on the days I can, I will fight it. Even when I am in that wheelchair or, on some days, trapped in this bed—no one can see it but me—but with every fiber of my being I am constantly waging a battle against this thief called multiple sclerosis. I have to.

Nearly every day I learn a little bit more about just how ruthless this ailment is. I don't talk about it—no one would understand. If you've never felt its sneaky grip on your limbs, pulling on you and pushing against your every move, it's not as though words can really convey the power of it all. It's an invisible prison—on a good day, it merely restrains. On a bad day, and trust me there are many, it's like a vise clamping on every muscle, every joint.

Most of the time, I try to let it have its way. But you better know that while it throws its violence onto my body I pray without ceasing. Because here's what I know about the Holy Spirit: Gratitude and grace go a long, long way. Sometimes I simply tune out everything and everyone around me and I start a prayer of thanksgiving. Even while people are talking and socializing all around me. That's right. I just get quiet. I am thanking God—rejoicing, in fact, in the Lord at the same time that MS is doing its thing. Maybe that seems strange, but not to me. For what you see here—the wheelchair and my sometimes-twisty limbs—are a "momentary light affliction . . . Look not only to those things that are seen" (2 Corinthians 4:17–18). Trust and believe I'm not looking only to those things that are seen.

And what I know is that there is beauty. I've always recognized beauty. Some people might think, "Oh, but you don't know fancy; you were born into a simple life in Buffalo—that is certainly not a place of beauty, with its factories and such." But they would be wrong. I can remember standing in awe, especially in downtown Buffalo, of the stately buildings. The way the city was laid out—I mean back when I was coming up. Surely you've heard of the great architect Frank Lloyd Wright. Goodness, his legacy is all throughout Buffalo. And the wonderful parks designed by Frederick Law Olmsted, the same beauty and wonder he bestowed on New York City's Central Park. I still smile when I think back to the Beaux Arts charm of my hometown, inspired the École des Beaux-Arts in Paris.

And even with all that the city began to lose in industry and wealth—we saw it happening, as youngsters, chipping away in the late 1950s—the city of Buffalo still had a warm, lovely spirit about it. The people believed in hard work and family. Our simple little flat was nothing to write home about on the surface. But my mother was a proud homemaker who raised me to appreciate the beauty in the simple things she was able to provide for us as a family.

It may sound trite, but beauty truly is in the eye of the beholder. The entities I love the most are quite simple. Beauty is all around. And I make sure to keep seeing it. We must.

I'm talking real and true beauty—like these pearls I put on every day. And I do mean: Every. Single. Day. It's part of who I am; it's who we all are. I think maybe I just like to remind myself more often than most. My earrings are right here on my bedside table, too. And I put them on—*with* my pearls—just as soon as I wake up. Jewelry and such, I know, most people consider accessories, right? These are things of beauty that mean a lot to me. Not as an add-on, an afterthought. Adornment is essential.

I'm telling you the truth—not just because I say so, as Marilyn Scales Underwood. Practically from the beginning of time, the ritual of meaningful ornamentation has been important. Read the history. Ancient Egypt, for example. Back then it would have been shells or maybe beads. Honoring the body with grace, culture, and spiritual significance. And you must understand: it's not about the earrings or the pearls in and of themselves. Heck, anybody can throw on something pretty—buy a lovely thing and wear it. No, anyone who thinks my pearls are merely my favorite style accent is suffering a grave misunderstanding.

They're missing the bigger picture. And I suppose there may be those who might say: "Oh, Marilyn is a sharp dresser. Her jewelry is pretty and so very tasteful." And I never really thought about it deeply but I suppose there may be some in the church who think the opposite.

A few who think, "That's not godly—that emphasis on adorning herself goes against scripture."

Nothing could be further from the truth. You know what the word says? God is not against beauty; that would be ludicrous. But he intends that we go deeper than mere superficial, fancy signifiers. The Bible tells us to revel in spiritual adornment—making your heart beautiful with hope, faith, joy, kindness, love, and things that are holy.

"Your beauty should not come from outward adornment, such as elaborate hairstyles and the wearing of gold jewelry or fine clothes. Rather, it should be that of your inner self, the unfading beauty of a gentle and quiet spirit, which is of great worth in God's sight. For this is the way the holy women of the past who put their hope in God used to adorn themselves. They submitted themselves to their own husbands, like Sarah, who obeyed Abraham and called him her lord. You are her daughters if you do what is right and do not give way to fear" (1 Peter 3:3–6).

It's no accident that I prepare myself—in and out—for the day. Each day you have to make time to do the things that make you remember who you are, okay?

Here's how my day starts. Usually I'm up before Frank. In easy reach, right there on my bedside table, my earrings and my pearls—single strand, because a little less is a lot more. Except when it comes to mascara.

I'm telling you what I know. This way you can appreciate a woman in your life. She may not have time for foundation. I mean, I make the time, but that's just me. But mascara is a must. Some powder, of course. And color, so the cheeks are rosy and healthy and vibrant. Now the lips should shine a bit.

Beauty is a blessing. Why wouldn't a woman want to honor that in herself? God gave us beauty. And I am not afraid to show it, to honor who and what He created me to be. And I'll tell you a secret. Everybody, and I do mean everybody, loves beauty. Yes, of course, it comes from within. But the wonder of being a woman is that we have the opportunity to highlight that inner beauty with a little bit of this and that on the outside as well.

We don't serve a happenstance God. He is very intentional in His creations. Women are not an accident. Not an afterthought. We are central to His vision on earth. The younger generation of women may feel the need to assert their importance, going out of their way *not to take* second place to a man. I tell you, it makes me laugh because if you study the word—it's clear how much women matter. So it's very important to take that to heart. Is it challenging? Absolutely.

Because how do I as a woman manage to be successful in motherhood—in the role as a wife—without losing parts of me? Tending to family can be all-consuming. No set hours—on call 24/7: cooking, bill paying, planning, shopping, cleaning, driving, all manner of care and feeding. And the physical demands barely scratch the surface. The real work is emotional, mental, and spiritual. You're pouring into others all day every day; and a lot of the time, you have to pour out whether your own cup is being filled or not. There are just so many needs. All. The. Time.

If I'm completely honest, I have to say that as much as I LOVE my family—they are the answer to my prayers, individually and collectively—I do struggle inside. I watched my own mother work so hard to care for me, as a single mom. It was just us two. But her life was filled to the brim with sacrifice. She had to be the nurturer and the breadwinner—with never a day, or even a moment, off from those tremendous duties. As a little girl, I longed for what I was missing. Not material things. Thanks to my mother's hard work, I didn't lack any of life's necessities.

But at night, I would lie awake, trying to imagine what it might be like if our family was—I don't know—different, with a mom and a dad. Many of my friends' families resembled mine. But I knew there were those that didn't. Families that looked more *Father Knows Best*, you know? It was idealized, of course, and I knew hardly anyone who lived like that in real life. Well, obviously you don't know the show. It was long before you were born, first a radio program—then on television. But you get the idea: nuclear, traditional. The lead character, Jim Anderson, was played by Robert Young, dashing at the time in a simple, down-to-earth kind of way, as the man of the house and so full of wisdom. Jane Wyatt had already been pretty established as a movie actress, and she played his dutiful wife, Margaret. They were solidly middle class. And when Jim came home from work, Margaret had everything together. The house was clean. She was dressed nicely, and so were the kids. They didn't have real problems, just cute little situations—like maybe if one of the kids slacked off on their chores, Jim would make a civics or life lesson or some such out of it. At the end of each episode, all of the day's issues were wrapped up in a bow—solved, of course, by Robert Young.

A huge part of me wanted that life. Clearly I couldn't have it as a kid. That ship had sailed. My dad was but a faded memory. He and mom couldn't make things work, and he wasn't a part of my life at all.

Don't misunderstand; we did just fine—Mother and I. My childhood was filled with love and laughter. Everyone in the neighborhood knew everyone else—we were one big extended family.

But the traditional setup, the all-American elements of that *Father Knows Best* life, tugged at me for I don't know how long. I always knew I wanted a real family-family. I knew the mom I'd want to be. And Frank is the husband I always hoped to have.

I'm blessed. And I know it. That doesn't mean I don't sometimes question—wonder—what if . . . Not *if* so much as *how*. What I'm saying is: Where is the balance? Or does a balance even exist? Now, today, as a woman—because, of course, I couldn't have known as a child, or even as a young woman working my dream career in fashion—I wrestle in my spirit a bit sometimes. I love my children, my husband, my life. I'd just wonder if there is a way to be all of me. The mother me. The wife me. The artist me. The thinker me. The spiritual me. The physical me.

At times it feels as though I've had to choose—lest risk denying my family what they need and deserve from me. It's a woman's natural instinct to give, I believe. Maybe it's just me. But pouring into another? It's almost reflexive. To feed. To serve. I also know that it's entirely possible that with so much time spent feeding, it's easy to forget your own hunger. It's the great paradox of being a woman. That's what that is. Then, suddenly—without warning—the hunger turns into starvation. And no little bite of food, or tangible sustenance, will do.

That's why I've had to understand over the years to still myself. Teach myself to be by myself—even if people are around. The thing is the soul needs solitude or it dies. So, whatever you do, remember you have to guard your heart; take care of your soul. Inner stillness is a must.

Solitude doesn't mean lonely.

This is what I had to learn. About life, my life. And it's not a simple thing to impart. But my most fervent prayer is that somehow I succeeded in teaching my children about that quiet, still place inside. Trust me when I tell you: That space is everything. Until you find it and tap into it, honor it, talk to it, listen to it, nurture it—you will never know peace.

And I don't say that lightly. How very easy it is for people in the world to look at us, see the things that surround us—things that symbolize success and achievement—then draw certain conclusions about us and our lives. You can't get distracted by that. Don't buy into it. There is, in fact, no amount of fame or fortune in this big ole world that can fill that quiet place inside you.

God put it there to remind us of who He is. And everything you experience is an outgrowth of that little space. It's where you summon discernment, wisdom—really, all good things. The word tells us: "Wisdom is worth more than silver; it brings more profit than gold. Wisdom is more precious than rubies; nothing you could want is equal to it."

Have you ever walked along the beach, just strolling along—and been stopped dead in your tracks by a gorgeous shell? Obviously, there are hundreds of shells lying on the shore. But somehow, some way, you happen upon one that stops you. Maybe it's broken. Maybe it's perfectly intact. But it grabs your attention—almost as though it is on the beach alone. See what I mean? It wasn't lonely.

Seashells are so fascinating to me. When you look inside, usually you see emptiness—when in fact something made a home in there, lived up in the two halves that got split apart. It's like that book I like so much. One of my favorite books, *Gift from the Sea* by Anne Morrow Lindbergh, talks about it all far more elegantly than I can . . . Almost anything about the sea just fills me with peace, soothes me. Because we like to think we have everything figured out—that we humans, in our very complex worlds, hold the answers. But we don't. The answers have already been made clear—and by way simpler creatures.

There is a poem I love so much. The Oliver Wendell Holmes one? It talks about the natural intelligence of the chambered nautilus. That's the name of the poem I think—"The Chambered Nautilus." The creature is not big at all but it lives way down deep in the sea and can make its own home—through struggle: "Wrecked is the ship of pearl! / And every chambered cell / Where its dim dreaming life was wont to dwell."

This little shell that most of us wouldn't think twice about can teach us all about struggle and how to survive. All these little compartments, sort of channels really, inside its shell—each one perfectly created to be a new home of sorts. That's strength, spiritual strength. You see the poetry of the pearl? It has beauty, and a toughness, at once. For the whole span of its life, the nautilus just keeps on keeping on.

Inside its shell—the outside world can't see—it's just as busy as can be, making the compartments so it moves in and out of them when it needs to. Just opening up one area to curl up in and then closing off another. Pretty clever way to do life, right?

I mean, the real point is that everybody's carrying something. No sense sitting around talking about what ails me. Like the Bible says, His "grace is sufficient." Right? Last night that tingling sensation in my legs came calling again. But I'm good. Really, it's more like burning. Very odd—nothing I've felt before—and bothersome because it wakes me from my sleep. Imagine hundreds of pins and needles jabbing through your skin—from shin to thigh? That's the only way I can think to describe it.

There are times when the pain won't let me rest. Those are the times I just lie here and I look up at the ceiling. And, depending on how bad the stabbing is pulsing through my body, I admit I sometimes have troubling thoughts. I just feel at times all the frustration welling up in my head. The thing is, I miss my life—the way it was before MS. I love my family and friends for seeing to my needs. Oh Lord knows, I'm so grateful. It's just that I want to get on by myself. The way I used to. I want to get up, get in the car, and drive myself to church, and resume my choir director duties. I want to see my friends for lunch, or maybe go shopping. I don't even have to buy anything—window-shopping was always so much fun.

Of course, I keep up with today's fashions. I read about this and that, love the magazine spreads. And I watch TV till I'm sick of looking at that box. Nothing can take the place of doing the actual living—no matter how entertaining some of the shows are. No one wants to hear these things. And I don't feel good even saying them to myself. I am so blessed. I know that. Really I do.

But I don't like living this way. I'm not sure I will ever get used to it. All the medicines I need to take certainly take the edge off, but I don't feel much like myself. That's the tradeoff. I'm quite sure no one would even guess that I have the kinds of thoughts I have during the night. These feelings are not like me—not like the mom the kids know or the wife Frank knows. But they are real. Honestly it's hard to describe them. You see, I'm convinced that it's just not good to have so much time being still, alone with your thoughts and your feelings.

After years and years moving all around the world as a military family and raising four children, all of this alone time is very new. I don't like it. I have so many feelings that I don't know how to process. Things will pop into my head from fifty years ago. There have been nights when in my dreams I see a near stranger, like maybe my dad—who, of course, I never knew as a young girl, although we did connect once I was grown—who has decided to come and sit on the edge of the bed as if to say, "Well, Marilyn, let's talk." Only, I don't know what to say. And I get lost in my head thinking, "Who are you?"

Sometimes I have thoughts that are unpleasant, often downright angry—if you want to know the truth. Not at God. Not at anyone, really. But the anger and frustration are there, so close I can touch them. And all those difficult feelings can keep me up all night.

Must be why I am so very tired some mornings. But, then, I've been tired for a while now. Seems like this bed does not want me to get up out of it these days. I know my friends and family worry about me. *Don't* is what I want to tell them. I'm okay. Really, I am. Tired is all.

Pearl of Wisdom

I had to learn to be alone—even when surrounded—because the soul needs solitude or it dies. Inner stillness is essential. That quiet space within? It's everything. Fame and fortune can't fill it. Guard your heart. Nurture your soul. Listen to that space—honor it. That's where discernment and peace live. God placed it there to remind us of Him. From that space, all good things grow.

My parents, Marilyn and Frank, on their wedding day, April 23, 1960, Buffalo, New York.

2

DEVOTION

I can hardly wait to celebrate. With the COVID bug going on, I know there is lots of confusion around the world right now. But this, too, shall pass. People will want to feel joy again. Frank and I will renew our vows at Gillfield Baptist Church. Won't that be lovely?

Yellow. They will all dress in yellow, like daffodils. Perfect for spring. Because, why not? Yellow, after all, is the color of optimism and creativity. Like the sun, yellow is cheerful and life-giving. I've had my eye out, and there's a place called David's Bridal—do you know it? I have never seen anything like that online store—I think of it as the Costco of weddings. I mean that website has nearly four hundred yellow dresses to choose from—what a selection!

I'll have a parade of bridesmaids, ten of them: including my two pretty daughters, of course; Timmye Yates—my dear friend from high school; Pam Sussman—who, like me, has been living with MS for years; Josie Hart and Veronica Dixon—Amway brought us together, but our friendship goes far beyond business. Frank and I were married on April 23, 1960. When I look back on life in those days it feels like a hundred years ago and yesterday at the same time. And I can hardly believe that we're coming up on our sixtieth wedding anniversary. He doesn't know it yet, but we are going to have the most glorious celebration he could ever imagine. This whole pandemic thing ought to be behind us by then. Of course, stay-at-home protocols are not new to me. I've *been* at home.

I can't get around like I want to in this chair with wheels on it. I'm a doer. I have always done things, gone places. When I pleased. With whom I pleased—or alone. I enjoy my own company, always have. God knows I love my family. I am so blessed by their devotion, their attention, their tender affection. There are no "buts"—it's only that I envisioned something different for myself, for my life. Frank and the children do everything—and I mean everything—they can think of to help make sure I do the things I love doing.

Truth is, no woman could wish for a husband like Frank. I don't think I could dream up such a model man if I tried.

This is an awful disease. But as challenging as MS is for me, it's also taken a toll on Frank. But you wouldn't know it. He never lets on. Just makes sure I have whatever I need at all times. And with a smile on his face. He is a blessing.

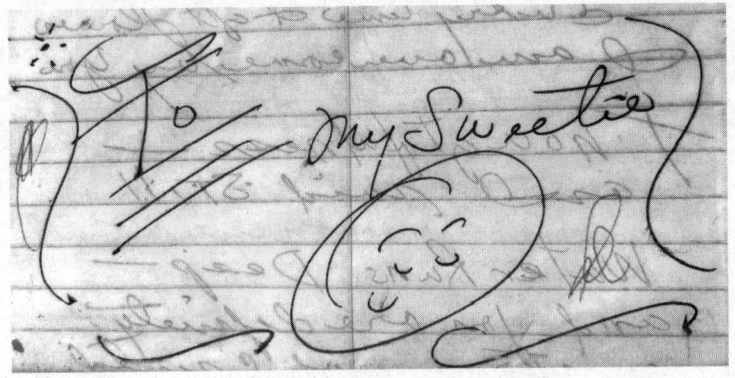

Mom's love note for Dad
Friday, February 18, 2005 @ 9:44 a.m.

Good morning.

I hope you know how much I love you and how much your loving and caring means to me. Who else would see me with short hair, a hair or scarf at night, a diaper plus change me all the time, to go shop for me. Buy nice . . . whatever you could afford, but always try to get what I want whether it's good for me or not, (like almond joys). But I think you did witness my fair well [sic farewell] to candy when you bought me four bars, although they were so good, I know now that sugar is bad for my immune system and MS is an auto immune disease, so I don't need to add to that. So Sweetie, I don't need any more sugar plus it may help the wheelchair to get lighter, so that I won't be any more strain on you putting me up and down the ramps. :-)

I know that you don't mind, but we both are seniors and whether we like it or not, we don't need too much body strain. I appreciate everything you do for me, but I want you to stay as healthy as you can, and I don't want my weight & my bad eating habits to contribute to any strain on you see, as I told you, The Holy Spirit talks to me at night, sometimes in my sleep, but like last night, I was wide awake all night and God told me wake up, stop eating things because they are good to you and eat them because they make you gain weight. Plus, the weight may make the chair too heavy for the love of your life. Be considerate, think that spelled right?

So! Before I get started today, please note, I'd like breakfast:-) one of the bratwurst sausages, grits, toast, plus a drink, please note if I have any of the tomato drink left look in the box on the floor in the dining room. Maybe two in there. If so, please empty, one carton in a glass, one lemon yogurt, two eggs plus blend them. Thank you. If no tomato juice is available, I will take one glass of milk, one yogurt +2 eggs. Thank you.:-) Need the two prescriptions you have for Linda and Dr Robertson's office!! You show them to Patti. I have not seen them since!!:-) I need them before I call Linda about my questions and statements and advice:-) Note! If you go upstairs for the prescription, please check my middle dresser drawer for my

- alert necklace.
- Brown card
- Beige alert button

Also need Q-tips. Please thank you, thank you:-)

I love you.

You are sooooo special:-) and as I said, before, when God made you, he threw away the mold.:-) You are some kind of man!!!

Have a wonderful day.

Marilyn. -over-

Now, is this poorly written letter better than un expensive card or not? Please note, quote from Marlo: "Mom I'm glad you're back, but I never thought you would return with a sense of humor." unquote.

Notice, the first five pages of this letter were written while I laid down. Look how much better I write setting up. Wow! Praise the Lord! Don't forget I love you:-):-) Marilyn -over-

Also, thank you again for my beautiful roses. Although they are not the same today, our love is, if not better.

Every time I get flowers, I am overcome by your

Thoughtfulness—and as I said, STILL water runs deep, and you are definitely a stream of crystal clear water, the kind you want to drink!!! And to think there was a time when I had nothing to say Ha!!!:-)

Let me tell you: I was a lovely bride. Of course, everyone told me so. But I was well aware—not because of my dress, my hair, or my makeup; the feeling came from the incredible joy of marrying the man of my dreams. And, oh goodness, if you could've seen the look on Frank's face. I believe he *knew* he was a lucky man. Do you hear me? We had decided to get married a few months earlier. Well, actually I'm the one who decided we'd get married, to be honest about it.

And it's actually funny because I had not been longing to get married at that point. Far from it. A friend had said a fella she knew was in the army and scheduled to come to Buffalo from Germany and would I be kind enough to introduce him to some young ladies. I thought, "Well sure, I'll be nice and I'll introduce him to a couple of my friends"—never knowing that this young man she was talking about was a wonderful, dashing, and grounded man who I would soon fall in love with. Anyway, he came to Buffalo, returning from his first Army assignment, and gave me a call. We decided to get together for lunch. His car hadn't arrived yet, so I actually picked him up—and I questioned at first whether that was really a proper thing to do. I did it, deciding that it was maybe a bit wild but also more or less permissible—since he wasn't someone I was dating.

I picked him up, and I really don't know what got into me. He got in the car, of course. And after we said hello and everything, my first statement to him was, "Well, I really don't want you to get interested in me." And he looked at me and his mouth dropped open and he said, "And who in the devil is going to get interested in you?" Well, I think he was really taken off guard because he had met a lot of young ladies in Germany and I don't know what they told him. But here he met someone who right away decided she wasn't fazed by him—his good looks, the uniform. I wasn't trying to play hard to get. I just felt I was fine by myself. And that was new; he didn't know how to take that.

All that to say that I cannot explain what happened to either one of us, because after that first meeting, we were seeing each other regularly. And I knew I wasn't going to just be spending my time with someone like that without some kind of intention. So I said, "Why waste time? We ought to get married." In three weeks we were engaged, and our wedding was three months later.

I had been going with someone in Buffalo for a little while—a young man I'd met when I was in high school. I liked him a lot. But, as my friends always said—and they were right: "Marilyn, he's all right, girl—but you can do better."

I knew Frank was my "better." I didn't know a whole lot about him at first. In fact, no one did. He was new to town. We didn't know his people or any of the kind of thing that, you know, usually you kind of use as a barometer of sorts. But there was just something to his almost regal countenance, you know. Immediately you could just sense his decency. There was no flash. And I will admit, the young Marilyn was sometimes drawn to style—that brand of confidence that wasn't exactly slick, but I guess you might say suave. That's the best way to describe it.

Frank had an easy smile. He was confident—didn't seem bothered by anything. Quiet in a way but also quick-witted. He was not only charming and handsome, but he also had substance. More important, I loved that Frank was a strong man of God. Now, I grew up in the church. I know the word. Seeing him teach Sunday school each week drew me to him. This is a man who could've been doing anything with his time on Sunday morning; and he chose to be in church—spreading the Gospel.

Everybody else knew one another in Buffalo. And when he started to teach Sunday school, naturally I picked up on the fact that this out-of-town guy hadn't been at the church for long. What no one knew at the time is that he was on a counterintelligence mission for the military. He was posing as a civilian, working in the post office building right downtown. There was a certain kind of mystery around him. He was a bit cool, handsome, very mannerable, and God-fearing.

We started to spend time together, went on some dates. And the truth is, the fella I had been seeing since high school wasn't about anything. He was the big brother of one of my high school friends. And I did care about him. I did. But we had been going together for a while—and, you know, nothing was moving in any kind of direction. Frank and I went to a few restaurants downtown, picnics, and other things.

I knew something was brewing, and he must've thought I was a pretty big deal—because he asked me to his office party. It was at his boss's house; and I think that was a signal in some ways. He knew I was someone who complemented him, added something. You don't take just anybody around your boss, someone you want to impress. That was a turning point in my mind; I do remember pretty well. What I felt in Frank's presence, especially that particular evening, was a sense of being both respected and protected.

Only thing—I know this sounds silly. But when I thought about getting serious with Frank, in my mind, there was one small drawback at the time: He drove this Volkswagen bug—they were becoming popular at the time. I owned my own Buick, so naturally you couldn't tell me a thing. Everyone I knew in Buffalo drove a Chevy or maybe a Ford. This funny-looking little car was weird to me. And, I remember thinking, "Why would a person own a car made outside the US? What does that say about a person?" I couldn't get the appeal of it to save my life. I started to like him, but I didn't like that car. And I told him so.

He said: "The car comes with me." Very matter-of-fact. He was very proud of that little car, I soon learned. It was German and he bought his *in* Germany. Not off a Genesee Street lot in Buffalo. What did I know? Only what I was accustomed to, right? It's not even like I'm some kind of car enthusiast. That lil' bug was just so peculiar.

So, he was clearly getting attached after a short time of seeing each other steady. And I didn't see where it made sense to keep courting. It was time to just settle things up. I wanted him to know I had no plans to just coast along. Mind you, we had been dating for all of about a month or so!

Once we decided, or I guess *I* decided, it was time to get married—I told him so one day. It was the middle of the week, and I think we'd just had a picnic in the park. We got engaged and set a wedding date roughly three months out. That weekend, I drove to New York City. The dress I wanted—there was a particular look already in my head—I knew where to find it.

Business trips to New York City were commonplace for me. And I knew quality and tailoring—fabrication, all of it. I'd been a buyer—coster is what it was called back then. I believe I was the first Black person hired at the company, in fact. I worked for Barmon Brothers; a team of seamstresses reported to me. At that time, we're talking about the 1950s and early 1960s, this was probably the largest dress manufacturer in the country. I even appeared in an advertisement in *Women's Wear Daily*. That fashion paper was a big deal—still is.

    See, I knew Lord & Taylor was having a sale. I knew how I wanted to look. I was to wear the dress; it wasn't going to be wearing me. I wanted lace, a detailed bodice. And I certainly had to have three-quarter-length sleeves. I wanted simple, sophisticated elegance. And that's what I got. My dress was marked down from $2,200 to $600. I bought it—and headed back to Buffalo. I was able to get some of the accessories in Buffalo, shoes and such. It was a daytime wedding. So that and the dress style dictated shortie gloves—you know at the wrist. It's a small thing, some people might say. But the truth is you don't wear opera gloves, the long ones, with just anything—or at just any time of day. You'd be surprised, but a lot of people don't know that.

    It was a lovely time. We planned a honeymoon in New York City, doing all the touristy kinds of romantic things one does: Radio City, the Statue of Liberty, Central Park. Mom and a few of them gave me a party, and I got dressed. Family friends made the food.

And Faith Missionary Baptist Church right there on Humboldt Parkway was the perfect setting for the ceremony. This was before the city stuck the expressway right through the middle of the Black community. Can you believe it? Just bulldozed all the lush beauty of the park to make a six-lane highway. It gets folks to the suburbs faster, I suppose. But at what cost? Such a shame. You know Buffalo's Humboldt Park was designed by Frederick Law Olmsted himself—same as Central Park. Buffalo was once a spectacular city—big enough to hold some opportunities, but small enough—especially for the Black people living there—to be in community.

It was a wonderful place to fall in love—to be in love. Of course, it didn't take but a minute for folks to see Frank for the good and noble man he is. Buffalo was a place of honest, hardworking people. Nobody cared about fluff and fancy airs. And with all the traveling he did—from city to city—what's the first thing Frank did? He found himself a church home. You see what I'm talking about? And led him to me. God at the center. The Bible says he who finds a wife finds a good thing. And, well, Frank is a godly man—he certainly knew what he'd found.

Our honeymoon was fabulous and full of energy in New York. Now, mind you—Manhattan had been my old stomping ground, when I lived at the Harlem YWCA and arrived to study fashion in Midtown. And I relished that time we had, with me showing him around and giving him a taste of all that I loved in the city. The shows, the hustle, bustle. Never for a second did I hesitate to show that side of me. He knew he was marrying a woman who'd experienced life, who had ambitions, dreams—a strong mind. Frank was not someone who wanted me to simply follow or fall back—in a demure, damsel kind of way. That's not to say I didn't submit to my husband. I do know God's word.

But Frank liked my strength—loved it in fact. It's so important that the person you love also loves all of you for who you are. He knew at once—we both did—that iron sharpens iron. He didn't have some super-fragile ego. Didn't try to dominate me. He wanted to partner with me. And I with him.

When we decided to get married, Frank's statement to me was: "I am in the Army to stay. Now, I love you, but if you don't want to travel and if you don't think you can cope with this life, let's call it quits now."

Is that somebody who knows what they want or what? So off we went, and it has been very exciting and rewarding ever since. We've been to twenty-two different cities. Living in Germany, I guess, for me, was the most exciting. And we just weren't there long enough. I guess we were there for about eighteen months. Frank's been there twice. But it was absolutely beautiful. It's great to get out of your environment a little bit—and not forgetting that you're American—but learning what other people are like, experiencing different cultures. And I think you also find out what you have at home and how great our country is. And it's a good experience.

Frank was a proud serviceman and he didn't need me to boost his ego. Early on, I took to military life. I don't know why or how. But despite some of the challenges, I loved the excitement. The new worlds. Certainly it was nothing familiar, not at all like growing up in a small city like Buffalo. We were real road dogs early on, I tell you. We traveled throughout Europe and just had the best time. We both have a sense of adventure, a love of life. After all, what did God put all of this beauty on earth for if not for His children to enjoy it!

I remember when we were in Rome. Imagine that. I had to absolutely pinch myself at times. Oh, I tell you, Italy is so very majestic—I just loved it there. And I nearly died and went to heaven when we met Mr. Bill Cosby and his costar Robert Culp there. I was thoroughly tickled because this was around the time Cosby was on television in a role that had nothing to do with his Blackness. *I Spy* really took off, and Frank and I were huge fans. Everyone was. Here was a talented Black man who'd really captured the attention of the entire country, someone doing so much for the race—making great strides in the world of entertainment. Naturally, this was way before any of the messiness that we've heard about him now, with allegedly abusing women and whatnot.

The 1960s were a very innocent time, in many ways. Not only in the country at large—but also in the armed forces. Young Black men, like Frank, were coming up into a world of opportunity with the ugliness of segregated forces behind us.

And I'd be careless not to mention what a striking figure Frank cut in his uniform, all starched and decorated. Mr. Cosby said he was honored to meet us. I know we were more excited to meet him. But he was very gracious and curious, too—about what Frank's work was like, how long he'd served, and such. Oh, that was a real highlight.

Look at how God works, will you? Now, all I knew for sure was that I'd fallen in love with a good man. I decided to follow my heart and move in the direction the Holy Spirit led me. Had I dreamed of leaving Buffalo and living a different kind of life? You better believe it. But in my wildest imagination I would never have seen myself seeing the whole world. It wasn't always glamorous; please understand.

And of course, we weren't rich. But we didn't need to be wealthy to enjoy the rich experience of travel. People may have assumed we had money. Really what we had was each other. And at the same time our journeys through Italy and Germany felt like magic, they also felt natural.

That's always been my prayer for my own children

when they decide to marry. It's nice if you can be with someone who can make you feel butterflies. Sure, that's lovely and very exciting. But not always. The key is to feel at home, completely at home and secure, in your own skin. That's what my husband has always done for me.

I have loved being his wife—even when it was difficult. And what I mean by that is Frank is duty bound: God and country. Know what I mean?

Oh goodness, I don't think I can ever forget when he was sent on that first tour to Vietnam in the Tuy Hòa Valley. Listen, he was ready to serve—to do what he had signed up for as part of the United States Army. But at that time, the country was very, very divided about the Vietnam War. There were protests everywhere. The young people were especially unhappy. The loss of life was staggering.

It was the early 1960s. And life was changing so fast. I could feel the whole world shifting in real time. The evening news could hardly keep up. Lots of young people were fired up against the war in Vietnam. Music on the radio was different; if you listened to the words they were protest songs. And they were becoming popular. Fashion was changing. Long hair, thigh-high hemlines—things we used to know were becoming brand-new. Russia and the United States were trying to beat each other to the moon, for goodness' sake.

John F. Kennedy had been elected president. He and

Jackie were very glamorous and youthful. Something like a quarter of a million people gathered for the March on Washington with Reverend Martin Luther King Jr. And Malcolm X went to Mecca and said when he stood before the creator he felt like a complete human being for the first time.

You could feel it—as though the country was moving far away from the past into a new era—for us as Black people, for women, arts, humanity. Of course, I was very young in those days. It was exciting, because my own life was changing as well. And I mean fast. In a short time I had gone from working in downtown Buffalo to being the only Black woman heading a department at Barmon Brothers Co. and, I'm sure, one of the few in the fashion industry. I lived at home with my mother when I met my husband. That's what young women did back then; there wasn't getting your own apartment so much. And Frank was a soldier's soldier. You know he is so honorable, right? The man he is now is the man he has always been. Once we married, I got pregnant that same year with Frank Jr. Then, three years later, I had Blair.

Frank is and always has been a man of duty—God and country, that's not a hollow phrase. He went off to serve, to fight. The bravery that takes is mind blowing when you stop to think about it. A proud officer there for his men. It was scary to me, of course, but he never hesitated, not one bit. There was no question that he'd go to Nam, that's what people called it. And me with being a new mother, well, Frank and I decided I'd stay in Buffalo rather than live on base. It was the right decision. I had help from Mother and my "village."

There are times in life, lots of times, when you look around and things might seem a bit frightening and uncertain and you have to work to stay positive. This was one of them. My new husband was nearly ten thousand miles away—in a place most of us had never heard of or knew anything about. It's so unlike anything today. There was no texting. No video to send. No email. Just long silence. Silence and prayers.

Frank was always thinking about us, though. And he tried his best to keep in touch—with what limited means we had back then. That meant recorded messages. He bought us a kind of tape recorder—a reel-to-reel player—before he shipped out. They were common in the military. And most businesses used them for dictation. It was huge, looking back. And actually, it was pretty fancy for the times. You would absolutely fall out laughing if you saw what it looked like. Talk about clunky. This was before eight-track, cassette, VHS, before all of that. I doubt you can find one on the market nowadays.

I can laugh now, but that reel-to-reel machine was a lifeline for me back in those days. See, when he could find some time, he would sit down and talk into the reel-to-reel in his office over there in Nam and make tape recordings for Blair, Frankie, and me. Then he'd send us the tape. Literally, that's what it kind of looked like—a spool of brown tape, just but so wide. Then it would come to our house in the mail. I'm making it sound fairly simple and straightforward.

But trust me. The whole rigmarole took a couple of months or so from start to finish. Let me tell you, each day I would stand in the window waiting for the postman—back then, the mail carriers were all men—watching like a hawk in case he had something for me. I had to trust God that my husband was okay. We all so looked forward to hearing his voice. My boys were too young to really understand where their dad was and why.

When that tape came, it was like Christmas morning. I would call Blair and Frankie into the house, and we'd all go into my bedroom. They would both climb up on our bed and scoot to get themselves comfortable while I got the reel-to-reel set up. Then: "Hello, boys, it's Dad calling." And they would both start grinning from ear to ear. He'd talk a little bit about fighting for our country. He'd give them both some special words about the importance of hard work and being good boys. Then, I'd quickly shoo them out of the bedroom so that we could have some time to ourselves—Mommy and Daddy talk is how I think I announced it. And the two boys would kind of roll their eyes and giggle.

They were both so fascinated and excited to hear

their dad's voice come out of that contraption. In fact my little ones were so excited that for a little while, all that Black boy joy made me forget the grave danger he was in. We deliberately played up the idea of adventure—that Dad was on the other side of the world for a noble cause. Something that was bigger than him, and us, and everyone. I'm quite sure both boys understood the notion of fighting. But, of course, Frank never focused on all the details of war—and, especially, not the unprecedented nature of the war in Vietnam.

The children didn't know that many American people hated the idea of the US military involved in some foreign battle with this enemy no one had ever heard of. People were angry about things going on in our own country. And they didn't like what they were seeing on the news every night. And, oh goodness, they were mad about the draft. And, Black people were upset that so many of our Black boys were dying. It was the first conflict in history where the armed forces were not racially segregated. That was a good thing, of course. But—well, it was all very complicated.

It was awful when we saw Frank off at the airport. Of course, I was worried and sad. But I couldn't let my boys see that. After all, Dad was off on an adventure—doing something very exciting. I put a smile on my face, and I worked so hard to think positively that I actually pretty much convinced myself for a time that *everything* was fine. It was going to be just fine. And it was going to stay just fine. The biggest challenge in that moment was distracting my boys. I didn't want them to see how some people were looking at their dad in his uniform. Some even jeered, like he was some kind of a traitor. They didn't care about our family or his heroism. And I had to do the best I could do to protect my young children.

News and information were nothing like things are today. No cable program, like CNN. We relied on the daily paper in the morning and, of course, Walter Cronkite in the evening. That's it. That's pretty much all we had to go on. And it did not look good. From our living room, that's for sure, things over there did not look good. And, of course, I knew my husband. I knew that if there was something he had to do to keep his men safe, that's what he was going to do. As for the jeopardy that put him in—he never let on in those reel-to-reel dispatches.

When I got the call, Blair and Frankie were outside playing. I think some way or another they had made up a game. And whatever the made-up rules were, young Blair objected strongly to the fact that his big brother was winning. That happened often, and I never got involved. So they were both surprised to see me come out to hush them. I made both boys come inside and sit down. And I believe they thought they were in some kind of trouble, because my tone was very serious. Of course it wasn't that at all.

I jumped right to it—said that Dad had been hurt over in Nam and he wasn't feeling well. I tried to explain that Dad might be "a little sick for a while," but was doing everything the doctors told him to so that he could get better and come home to us as soon as possible. I didn't even mention the words *gun* or *shot*. Blair wasn't but about four or five years old. And he had a very worried look on his face, so I tried to compare the war injury to the time he'd fallen on the concrete and bloodied his knee. I said, "Remember, son? It hurt at the time but now look—you're good as new."

Of course the three-year age difference between Blair and Frankie revealed itself. Frankie had lots and *lots* of questions. He wanted details: Did the bad guys shoot dad? Did they have machine guns? How many tanks do they have over in Vietnam? Is he really going to be okay?

I made sure they both believed Dad was fine. But the truth is, I had to convince myself. And it wasn't easy. This life I'd signed up for, as a military wife, was still very new to me—and challenging. Back then, the army gave us wives a few booklets of information about a whole range of topics. But I was clueless about the details, the risks, the danger much of the time, especially once Frank was deployed.

Sure, I knew he boarded an airplane. And I knew the plane was bound for Vietnam. But once he left my sight, I had no way of knowing he'd arrived safely. No idea where he was exactly or what his mission was about. That's true for all military wives, but I was in the dark even more than most. You see, everything about Frank's career was covert because of his standing as a counter-intelligence special agent. Even when we'd started dating, it was some time before he told me that he wasn't really a Buffalo postal worker. That was just a foil for the mission he'd taken on. With Buffalo being so close to the Canadian border, I guess it was a good, low-key place to operate from while he conducted whatever international spying mission the army had going on back then.

Naturally I knew enough to be concerned when we found out he was going to do a tour in Vietnam. Looking back, a lot of it was unclear. I mean, to me—as a civilian. And knowing Frank, he wouldn't have shared details of his unit and its operations even if he could. He didn't want me to worry. And he has always been a "duty first" soldier. The oath? It's far more than a string of words to Frank. He lived up to that pledge: *I do solemnly swear that I will support and defend the Constitution of the United States against all enemies, foreign and domestic; that I will bear true faith and allegiance to the same; and that I will obey the orders of the President of the United States and the orders of the officers appointed over me, according to regulations and the Uniform Code of Military Justice. So help me God.*

It was only a few months or so into the tour when Frank got wounded. There was a little bit of information given to me. It was a very formal and succinct notification. I received word of the injury from an Army official. That was the protocol. It's against the rules to go into particulars during that formal notification. The point was to advise families of their loved one's health. It would've been a different kind of call if he were dead, of course—or really close to death.

They shared just the broad strokes: a leg injury. That little bit of information was a big relief. I knew that most combat deaths came from head and neck wounds. It didn't seem like it at the time, but in hindsight Frank's leg wound was a kind of blessing. So many were killed in combat. The Vietnam War was a very, very long and tragic time. I learned much later that we lost nearly sixty thousand troops; and the number of wounded troops was about three hundred thousand. Remember that sitcom *M.A.S.H*? M.A.S.H. means Mobile Army Surgical Hospital. Alan Alda played Hawkeye, and he was terrifically funny. Odd, in a way, that it was so popular—given the subject matter.

M.A.S.H was set during the Korean War, and Nam was still ongoing; it was a silly show in a lot of ways. But it was that kind of military medical operation that kept Frank alive and helped save his leg. Only once he got back home did I fully understand how badly Frank had been hurt. There had been a terrifying sneak attack—a fiery explosion—and the grenade detonated just as he lay resting in bed. Frank said his left leg was blasted so badly it looked like hamburger meat! Can you imagine?

With a host of injured troops Frank was airlifted to Japan to a facility where he got the best care available. It was a slow and difficult recovery. And I thank God he didn't lose his leg altogether. It's a miracle really. I'm so grateful Frank got the rest he needed—although I missed him terribly. And naturally, as his wife, I wanted to be there by his side, helping him heal and supporting him. Thank God, he was being cared for by the USO. Frank was with hundreds of other men at one of their operations in Japan.

And this is where the story gets really good. Hollywood stars would often pay visits—live performances, camp shows—to the troops to help boost morale, and as a way to say "thank you for your service." Remember, the entire country back then would enjoy those Bob Hope specials. They were huge. Maybe, in a way, like reality TV is now. Well, Frank was entertained by several popular celebrities during his stay there as well.

Very different times back then, let me tell you. Pretty much anyone who was anyone was honored to pay their respects to servicemen and servicewomen. It was a highly patriotic thing to do, and culture—as a whole—was happy to show their American pride. So those USO performances drew the likes of Sammy Davis Jr., Ann-Margret, Redd Foxx, Lola Falana. Stars among stars of that era.

Now, Frank is in no way as taken with celebrities as I am. He doesn't remember the names of who starred in what. But during one of those USO entertainment nights, he and one *major* actor, in particular, struck up a conversation. Frank was asked about his family and such. He says it was very meaningful and sincere. He quite enjoyed talking to the gentleman.

Trust me. Nothing could've prepared me for the phone call I received weeks later. In a very distinctive and resonant voice—just like you'd imagine Moses would sound; he was so good in *The Ten Commandments*—the man on the other end of the line said: "Hello, I'm Charlton Heston. I met your brave husband, Frank Underwood. He told me to tell you he is doing just fine and he loves you and the boys with all of his heart."

You know you could've knocked me over with a feather—I mean, Charlton Heston!

Pearl of Devotion

Oh goodness, if you could've seen the look on Frank's face—he knew he was a lucky man. What I felt in Frank's presence was a sense of being both respected and protected. Frank liked my strength—loved it in fact. It's so important that the person you love—love all of you for who you are. He knew at once—we both did—he wanted to partner with me. And I with him.

Mom in Colorado Springs, Colorado, 1973.

3

DISCIPLINE

Believe me when I say, I was always cleaner than the board of health. Every day. High school was a time when I began to really feel as though I was about to enter the adult world—and do adult things, have a career and a family. I had a pair of kitten-heel shoes. Very ladylike. I carried what we called an attaché case—you don't really see them anymore nowadays—and I had a clipboard. I don't quite remember the reason why, but I wanted to be prepared to jot down important information, and I suppose I thought it was more professional-looking than a plain student notebook. Even then, sixteen-year-old Marilyn wanted to stand out—make a statement. Not only with my appearance but also with my attitude. Everything needed to say: "Make no mistake: I'm ready."

Education was not something that Black people could take for granted. My friends and I—most everyone I knew, actually—took life and opportunity very seriously. We were determined to be *somebody*. Whether it was my one girlfriend Timmye, who was studying hair and cosmetology, or the other Marilyn, who was into business. Girls High School, near downtown Buffalo, was a place we were all proud to attend. Vocational training is what it was. And that was new for young women at the time.

This was the 1950s. The school majors broke down into areas like business, advertising arts, fashion, and so on. The message we received as young girls—young Black women—was "the sky's the limit." We believed it. Along with our trade studies, some ladies took college entrance courses. It was an integrated school, and I can't recall any racial issues. I was closest to the young Black girls who lived near me—we'd known each other since grade school. We were confident, and we looked out for one another. We were going places. That, we were sure of. Why? Because, quiet as it's kept, Buffalo had been a mecca for Black families from the South especially during World War II, where wartime factories such as Bell Aircraft and Bethlehem Steel needed all hands on deck in the war effort, and it mattered less the color of the hands. Word of mouth spread throughout the South, and thousands of families migrated to Buffalo, whose historic frigid winters could stiffen the spine of all who dared to put down stakes.

Folks worked hard, and even as teenagers so did we. We had part-time jobs. Everyone knew not to trouble our parents for spending change. We wanted to help out. A few of us worked at the local hospital, Meyer Memorial. And I did, too, for a time. It was school, work—then school and work the next day. Nobody was lazy, not one of us. We would make our clothes look as fine as possible. Dress patterns were a few cents apiece. Then we'd buy fabric. Didn't need but a yard or so. We could swing that. Barbara was the one with real sewing skills. And she might help us make an outfit here or there. But thankfully, we were mostly wearing the simple, classic sheath-type dress. Straight up and down, two pieces of fabric, front and back. A woman can never go wrong with simple. Instant elegance. See, then we'd each give it personality with accessories. Timmye would make sure our hairstyles were laid just so, our eyebrows were tweezed. Oh, she knows beauty—always did.

Everything is casual today, so I guess it's hard for young people to imagine. But back then we were committed to dressing up and stepping into the life we were planning for ourselves. Now, of course, no one had much money. I'm not talking about fancy, we weren't turned out in expensive finery. Just styling—the best way we could. Dignified. Timmye, Barbara, Lenore, and me—our backgrounds were similar. At our house, it was Mother and me—her only child—and I could see how hard she worked to take care of me.

She worked from job to job and did her level best to take care of me. As a very young girl, I had no clue what went into raising a child. And I can remember putting her through a lot of changes when I was about ten or so—pestering her about why I couldn't have a closet full of frilly dresses like my neighbor may have had or why I didn't have this and why I couldn't have that. At that age, there is no concept of things like sacrifice and paying bills. All you know is "I want," and it was only years later when I finally realized what Mother had gone through alone. At one point she was a nurse's aid. She also worked the elevator at Lerner's Stores building. The fashion girl in me was excited by that job. Maybe it wasn't a glamorous task, but in my mind, it was close to glamour. From a young age, I don't know what it was, but I loved high style. We may not have had much growing up, but I never felt deprived or that I lacked anything. I never, for one minute, doubted that I would one day be surrounded by more fashionable items than my eyes could hold.

When I say that, some people may feel that my thinking comes from a place of arrogance. Quite the opposite. My words were born out of faith. I'm not talking about tangible beliefs on style and grace, although I knew I'd have some of that, too. The Bible says, "What no eye has seen, nor ear heard, nor the heart of man imagined, what God has prepared for those who love him."

I had a vision of my future.

Always.

Some might say that vision maybe looked unrealistic, pie in the sky. That kind of hopeless thinking is so small—I mean, it's beneath any of God's children.

When I was growing up, my modest house was filled with love. We lived downstairs in a two-family house that was comfortable, with food always in the cabinets and all that we needed. My mother doted on me; and she gave me a strong, Christian foundation. Now, we had fun times as well. I simply knew my life as an adult would look different. I knew I'd have a wonderful, kind, and handsome husband—that I'd have beautiful children and a nice home.

Did I know how it would happen?

Of course not.

But I didn't fret. We don't serve a God of fear.

For a number of reasons—not least of all finances—I knew there was no way I would be able to go to college. But Mother often said, "If you really want to become a fashion designer, I'll do my best to support you."

And that was great. Looking back, now that I'm a parent, I wonder: What did she go through, knowing she didn't have the money to do a lot of the things a child would want, or even need? I'll never know, but what I do know is she always found a way to make magic happen. Once, she presented me with a challenge: If I worked for a year, and saved my money, she'd match what I had.

A bold proposition, indeed, because, of course, we still had bills to pay; and it wasn't as if she earned enough money to have any kind of surplus. And I said to myself, "Now, if she can do that, I know I can do my part," and I wasn't going to let her down. And so right after high school, I started working in a factory making custom drapes for the department stores. That's a valuable trade to learn, and now I really appreciate having that skill—I can admit, it didn't mean much to me at the time though. It's nice to know that I can do it if I want to; not a lot of people can. But I worked for a year, just as we'd bargained, and when the time came, I was ready to go away to school.

All I wanted to be was a fabulous fashion designer. I would just go to bed at night and lie dreaming about how great it was going to be. And I was going to go to Paris and I was going to be this, and I was going to be that, and I would see this, and do that. And Mother always encouraged me. She was as excited as I was—and really believed I would be successful. Going to New York City, traveling nearly five hundred miles by bus—leaving behind Mother, my home, my friends—it never occurred to me to worry or be afraid. I was so naive. What could go wrong? We always focused on the positive. Dream, and dream big. I was blessed to have the kind of mother God gave me, who let me follow my heart. When I first told her about going off to New York, she barely blinked. I know now, as a mom, she surely had some concerns. But she never let it show.

Her philosophy was: Work hard for what you want in this life. I realize now, she was teaching me something very valuable. And I've tried to do that with my own children: Put some skin in the game. I can remember when Blair was maybe fifteen or so and decided he wanted to be an actor. I drove him and his sister to the local dinner theater—it's still around to this day: Swift Creek Mill Theatre in South Chesterfield, Virginia. Of course, it wasn't Broadway. It was a local dinner theater. But the word says "do not despise small beginnings" does it not? I told him to go inside and see if he could get an acting job. He looked at me and said, "Okay, you're coming with me right?"

And I said, "No, son. This is on you." He was in that theater office for some time. I started to get a little anxious for him. Then he came bursting out of the building with the widest smile. And Blair was a genuine paid actor from that moment—working nights and weekends in production after production. So was Marlo; she is very talented as well. They both played in *Finian's Rainbow*.

My mom presented an amazing act of trust by forcing

me to stick my neck out. That's where I learned most of my mothering instincts. What she proposed sounded like a very fair deal.

Of course, it was a different time. For Black people it was as though the world was just beginning to open up. And we were all so happy for any and every opportunity that came our way. Life wasn't as complicated when I was growing up. So my day-to-day experiences felt very straightforward. Sometimes there's a grace and an ease to being naive. Trust me, we were all naive in many ways back then. We didn't know to be scared or intimidated. What I knew was that the Traphagen School of Fashion was renowned. If I was going to live out my designer dreams it seemed quite natural to me that to be the best, I had to be trained by the best. And I planned to be the best.

Traphagen had turned out American fashion greats, such as Geoffrey Beene and Anne Klein. Arthur McGee, who got less recognition than the leading white designers in mainstream fashion, was another graduate. He was an extremely talented Black fashion designer to Lena Horne and other celebrities. McGee and Ann Lowe, who designed Jackie Kennedy's wedding dress, were essentially the Jackie Robinsons of fashion. Once settled in at Traphagen, I worked very hard to soak in all my lessons and loved every minute.

For me, the biggest challenge was not the instruction.

I was always a worker and poured my whole self into each course, learning about color and motifs. Hands-on study was my favorite, but I enjoyed other subjects, including the philosophy of fashion. It was all entirely fascinating—because as a youngster all I knew was that I loved fashion and creativity. To hear the science behind it though? And the history? Amazing! And we learned about how fashion needed to be adapted to American lifestyles. That it wasn't enough to design some beautiful piece—but that it had to be accessible to regular people and fit their needs.

After a full day of classwork I would return home uptown to Harlem with my head dancing from everything I'd just learned. Mind you, although New York City was a long way from the Deep South, I did have a time finding a place to live—lodging that was safe, that I could afford, and that rented to Blacks. God was with me, because I ended up taking a room at the Harlem YWCA on 137th Street. I loved that it was a Christian-run organization. But it was far more than simply a place to live; it was a vibrant and welcoming community. At that time many Harlem folks called it the "little Y," a reference to its "little-sister" status to the much larger YMCA men's facility around the corner.

I didn't know it then—in fact, I had no clue—that a long line of highly esteemed Black women had lived in those same quarters before me. The historical significance is something that to this day astounds me. It was years before I'd realize all the important things that were created by Black people in those few short blocks of Harlem. The intellectuals, the Civil Rights heroes, the artists.

Greatness is in all of us. That's why I will always say to my children and my children's children: Walk in your greatness, child. All of us, especially as a race of people, are living history every day. Make it so. Be a testament. Honor God with your very best effort in whatever it is you choose to do.

In the 1920s and 1930s greats such as Pauli Murray, Leontyne Price, and Dorothy Height lived in that same Harlem YWCA building. I bet they didn't know then the legacy they'd be leaving for generations to come. And just around the corner, the YMCA—steeped in so much Black accomplishment.

Folks called it the "living room" of the Harlem Renaissance for goodness' sake. Langston Hughes lived there, Ralph Ellison, Claude McKay, and Jimmy Baldwin all lived there at the peaks of their creativity. And there was the Y's "little theater" program, which helped launch Cicely Tyson's career, Paul Robeson and James Earl Jones.

So now, then. Imagine me—Marilyn Scales from Buffalo living and breathing all that Black talent. I loved New York City. The energy. The people. Even the craziness of it all. It was pure theater on those streets. And to me, then and now, American theater was the highest art form ever.

There was certainly no Broadway theater in Buffalo. But I knew and appreciated the classic artistry and wonder of shows like *The King and I*. See, life was very different back then. I know that nowadays, sure, Broadway theater is respected. But throughout the 1950s, those musicals were the heartbeat of popular culture—even if I hadn't seen the shows. The way young people lie in wait for a Beyoncé album, we held our breath for the next stage musical. Those songs were our pop tunes, the music that we all wanted to lose ourselves in.

Back home, I'd listen to the show tunes and piece together the stories—know what I mean? Rodgers and Hammerstein were our Motown. Songs from *The Sound of Music* were the soundtracks of our lives. Of course I didn't know it at the time, but what I was witnessing was the Golden Age of Broadway. Well, from the sidelines at least. Naturally, I couldn't afford to actually see any of the shows, and to this day I'm not even certain I could've—as a Black woman. As crazy as it may sound by today's standards, I never even thought about it. I'd never even dreamed of attending a Broadway show.

But I must admit, inside my heart of hearts I entertained the idea of being onstage. Mind you, I've never had any drama coaching. And my exposure to theater really went only as far as the show tunes I loved listening to on the record player. Still, I dreamed of walking onstage and playing a role of some kind. It may seem silly, but for some reason I never lacked confidence. And in my mind I was surely leading lady material.

But honestly, my studies consumed me. And I was so grateful to be in the center of it all. New York City captured my imagination, that's for sure. So much excitement that your entire body is just filled with a sense of opportunity. A simple ride on the subway packed more energy and electricity than I'd encounter in a year being in Buffalo. It was fifteen cents back then. And you got far more than a ride to your destination.

For a creative person there is simply no better place to be than New York City. And fashion? Forget about it! There were, of course, the fashion principles I was learning every day at this esteemed institution. We were taught what Traphagen was known for back then: an American aesthetic. I would write letters home to tell Mom all of the great things I was learning, doing, and seeing. She was thrilled for me. I know she was. Just my leaving Buffalo for New York had made her so proud, And to see how I was growing and coming into my own.

As a mother, that is the ultimate dream—and as your child grows into adulthood, there is an enormous pride that goes along with that. But we have to remember: I was an only child. My dad was not in the picture. I was essentially all she had. So the pride was tinged with a touch of sadness. A longing that she never spoke but I sensed. The letters from her never closed without a "Can't wait to see you" or a "When you come back home . . ."

I just thought New York was the most fabulous place on the earth. And after I finished school, I started working, I guess, for four or five months as an assistant designer. And that was kind of nice, and I thought, "Okay, that's just one step up, and next I may move into being a head designer." Of course, it doesn't happen as easily or as quickly in real life as it does in our imagination. There were definitely times when I felt a bit discouraged and lonely. And in between there somewhere, my mother really missed me and started feeling like, "Well, I'm here in Buffalo alone and you're in New York alone, why don't you come home?"

Looking back, we were all we had—Mother and me—in the whole world. I missed her terribly; even at my loneliest I really was not ready to leave New York City. But I felt like I had to take her feelings into consideration as well. I didn't want to hurt her. So I said, "Mom, I'll come home Easter Sunday and I'll look for a job on Monday. And if I don't find a job by three o'clock on Monday I'm going back to New York." Well I went down to the employment office, and the woman who had helped me get my first job said: "You're not gonna believe this, but there is one large dress firm in Buffalo. And they have one job open."

She felt that I had all the qualifications—and wanted to send me out on an interview with the company right away—but admitted she wasn't exactly sure what I'd be doing. I didn't have anything to lose, really, so why not go on and check it out? You ever go somewhere to look for a job, and hope they say no? That's how I walked into the interview at Barmon Brothers. Do you know I didn't even take my sketches or anything, I just wasn't that interested; it was something I was doing for my mother.

I can't even remember what I said, but they told me I had the job—then asked, "Can you come back this afternoon and bring your sketches?" I was gobsmacked. I said, "Sure." Then I met the boss, and we really clicked. His family had owned this firm for thirty-five years, and they made daytime dresses and golf dresses and so forth. And he told me that the woman who I was to replace had been working there for thirty years. She was top in the field, he said—cost and estimating, designing, the whole ball game. But after a disagreement she'd decided to retire and refused to train anyone.

Anyone who knows me knows how I am all about a challenge. To me, it's like an invitation. He said if I was a self-starter and willing to take on the challenge of learning this whole thing from the shipping room all the way up to production, it was going to be worth my while. How could I say no?

This was in 1958. They had about six hundred employees. And they had never hired a high-level Black person. Well, there were about twenty-five women that had to work for me. And they decided they weren't going to listen. Oh, did they ever put me through it! In their minds, I suppose, they saw no point in taking direction from me. Race was obviously a factor, and they probably held some affection for the person I replaced, and that was another huge challenge. It wasn't easy at all. So I prayed a lot that first year. And eventually I think a lot of people found out that if a woman—a Black woman, at that—knows her stuff and gets a shot, she can do a fantastic job. They found that out, and it worked well for me. And when I left there, the same women who had given me a really hard time the first year were the same women who gave me two bridal showers—like a complete set of china—and they just had changed their whole attitude, because they learned firsthand what can happen if a person who might be different is given half a chance. And that was quite an experience. I was there for a good four and a half years.

During this time, several friends—I guess about four sets of friends—had gotten married. And they all started feeling sorry for "poor old" Marilyn, because Marilyn was twenty-four and Marilyn wasn't married. Now, mind you, Marilyn wasn't upset at all. I thought I was a big deal, in fact: I had a Buick; and I had money in the bank; and I looked half-decent. I wasn't worried about anything.

My career was very, very gratifying. I fully expected to struggle a bit to find work opportunities. I mean, Buffalo—no one has ever thought of it as "fashion central." But back then, with its ports along the Great Lakes, it was an important part of the country's economy, a place where all kinds of shipping and production originated.

Barmon Brothers Co. was the industry leader in what most of us would now call housedresses. Across the country, it was really a staple of a lady's wardrobe—at the time, of course, most women were homemakers. I was hired, and in no time I was leading a department and supervising a team of seamstresses. Words alone cannot begin to express how proud that made my family and friends. It was a very big deal. And I knew it. Most of my workers were Polish women who'd grown up sewing back in their home countries. After a rough start, I know they respected and appreciated me for my hard work.

I've seldom been naive—and especially in the 1950s, Black people were not given a fair shake in this country. But I made sure to do everything in my power to prove myself—at all times. With a strong work ethic and a positive attitude, I'm convinced we can turn most any hardship around. That was ingrained in me and everyone I knew. Hold your head up—nose to the grindstone—and keep on keeping on. That's how success is made, doing just that from one day to the other. And before you know it, you've built a good life for yourself.

When I was introduced to Frank, one of the most pivotal connections we made was based on the principles of hard work. Yes, of course I had a lot of respect for the service he committed to our country. And I appreciated the fact that he was a God-fearing man—humble and gracious. But I really fell in love with the way he talked about his future—well, his and soon-to-become ours. It was not a happenstance or wishful perspective. No, not at all. He was very clearly a man determined to take on the odds, squarely size up a strategy, and forge ahead.

To this day, I so admire that quality. And I am grateful that as partners, and then as parents, we were completely aligned. Nothing was halfway. We both have always been of the same mind: Despite prejudice and seemingly unfair circumstances, you find that greatness inside of you—because it's definitely there; we serve an abundant God—and go for it.

His high ranking in the military, he always said, was the direct result of his attitude. His deeply profound belief in his own leadership skills. Now, he was a great athlete at his high school in Steubenville, Ohio. It's easy to think the football field is where he got that sense of self-assuredness. But Frank has always been multifaceted. There's a story he sometimes tells of being in a school of mostly whites and getting an assignment to write an important essay.

Now he was a young teen at the time, and he really didn't feel as though his work would gain much notice from the teacher. He hadn't thought of himself as a great student, just one who worked hard. That essay earned him one of the highest grades in his class. And it was a real turning point. Later that year, he ran for class president of his mostly white high school, and won! He just led in so many areas on and off the field that it became second nature for him to expect to do well. That inside him were God-given strengths.

He used to say too many people today hold back—they don't *think* they have what it takes. But it's there, even if you have to dust it off or maybe polish it. Now that doesn't mean you won't be challenged—you've gotta prove that it's there. But that's nothing to shy away from, and you can't let it deter you.

Do your part, Frank says that all the time. If you're positive enough you will be that person; you'll get that promotion, that assignment you are going after. Claim it. That's what it takes to be successful, you see. When you set that intention as the purpose in your life, success does not deny you. It doesn't dare deny you. There will be a price—and you have to be willing to pay the price. But the success will come.

Pearl of Discipline

*I took life and opportunity very seriously.
I had a vision of my future.*

Always.

If you're positive enough you will be that person; you'll get that promotion, that assignment you are going after. Claim it. That's what it takes to be successful, you see. When you set that intention as the purpose in your life, success does not deny you. It doesn't dare deny you. There will be a price— and you have to be willing to pay the price. But the success will come. Greatness is in all of us.

My mom, Marilyn, and my dad, Frank Sr., standing behind her while at an event at the Woman's National Democratic Club, Washington, D.C., August 26, 2022.

4

PERSEVERANCE

I mean it's not like I couldn't function. At least at first.
Yes, I occasionally had trouble seeing. But, at the time, I just didn't think it was that big of a deal. That sounds odd, right? Some things you just push aside. At the time I thought it was minor—nothing I was going to let get in the way of our family.

There was some headache pain here and there. Who hasn't had headaches? Especially mothers. Come to think of it, sometimes my eyes would hurt a bit, too—something I thought had to do with the headaches. You know how some headaches start here—right at the temples—then it sort of moves, right? I never mentioned it to anybody. I thought it would pass. And most of the time it did. I remember the very first time—not because it was the worst, but it had me so darned confused and frustrated.

We were living in Colorado Springs, I think, one of the first times it came down. I mean, the blindness. I realize now that's what it was—with all that the medical experts now know about multiple sclerosis. Back then—we're talking 1975, maybe? No one knew all that much about it. At the early onset of the MS, the optic nerve can swell up to the point of blindness. In a million years, I would've never called it that. Blindness? It sounds so—I don't know—just not me. If there is anything I can do—it's see. Part intuition. Part good sense. Part Holy Spirit. I could always *see*. And see things no one else could. Even if it affected only my physical ability and not my discernment. No—just no. I rebuked that. Quick, fast, and in a hurry.

And at first, it lasted just a little while. Colors weren't so vibrant. In fact, things would seem to go gray all of a sudden. Things I knew to be bright red—like the choir robes at church—went dull. Like somebody had put a dirty filter on a lens. I knew something wasn't right. But in that moment? I brushed it aside. What mattered right then and there was getting the alto section to come in and hit that space under my sopranos. I loved that little church, but the choir was probably one of the more challenging I had worked with over the years. Great voices, that was for sure. But the harmony. That's where I had to really bring them along. And every week, they looked good. Each one. Instinctively I knew whatever seemed amiss was me—not the choir, not the robes. But I wouldn't admit it. Not even to myself.

And when I think back, it scared me. It really did. After service ended, we went home. I no longer had the same distraction as the choir's lagging altos to take my mind off my vision problem. I had a household to run. By that time three children and a husband meant a ton of activity. Sundays were full. Every week. But as demanding and jam-packed as the activities were each Sunday, I looked forward to each one.

Church was always central to my very being. And moving to a new city every two years with Frank's military assignments made it even more so. I mean, yes. The pastor and the congregation at every base were different from the last. And, of course, I had my favorites. And my not-so favorites. But it was still the Word of God. And hymns in Colorado Springs were the same hymns as in Fort Benning, Georgia.

That first time my eyes started playing tricks on me, I knew it was nothing I had time for. And I told God, "I need you to make things right—can't nobody else do it but you." At the time, I had never heard of MS—let alone know about any of the symptoms. It would be nearly twenty years before I learned that I was experiencing optic neuritis. How do you like that?

Apparently, this nerve that controls vision has a fine coating—like the lining of a well-made coat, know what I mean? And when multiple sclerosis starts to set in, it somehow gets to breaking down that lining. I was a textbook case—symptoms like mine play out for something like 70 percent of people with MS. And a lot of times, this optic neuritis thing is the first MS sign they have. But, like me—especially back then—most of us don't know it. It can start out like a smudge—as if fingerprints on a pair of shades mucked up what you were seeing. So you see, but in a blurry way. Colors fade and whatnot. For a whole lot of people, there's a good deal of pain that comes along with it.

That first time I don't think I had really bad pain. I mean I'm not sure. Mostly it felt to me like I had a headache that wouldn't let up. But I got through it—faded colors, blurred vision, and all. Sunday dinners were a big deal. It didn't really matter what shade of red or pink the raw beef chuck was, it braised the same. That's the way I thought about it. A little eye trouble wasn't going to get in the way of me mincing the garlic, cutting carrots, chopping onions, or searing that meat the way I needed to. After all, Sunday dinner wasn't going to cook itself.

The next day, I'd decided I was going to see like normal. This nonsense with all the bright colors around me bleeding as though I'd put a new pair of dungarees in the wash with whites was starting to get under my skin. Even though it wasn't stopping me from doing the things I had to do, it was unnerving. I wanted to be done with it all. But it wasn't done with me, I guess. It was about two weeks or so before I could really see straight.

I never said a word—didn't want Frank to worry. He had so much on him already. It wasn't wartime, but that didn't mean he didn't have a ton of responsibility. All of his men depended on him. And he never said it, but I know he felt some pressure as a Black colonel to be better than all of the other officers. I was determined to make things as easy for him as I could.

The other officers' wives—all white—were enormously social. There was a luncheon this week. A tea party next week. And so on. Always something. And don't get me wrong, the ladies were just lovely. They really were. So warm and so gracious. They'd make such a fuss over my decorating.

With each move, every two years, I would think about what I wanted the theme to be. In Colorado Springs, I made harvest-gold drapes. That shade was all the rage back then. But I did it at a high level, with textured fabric. Without layered fabric, the whole look falls flat. Know what I mean? It was a blessing that I had that drapery job after high school at Rosenfeld's back in Buffalo. You know they were one of the leading home decor manufacturers in the country. Truly, right there in Buffalo. Hard to believe, right?

I learned everything at Rosenfeld's, all the details of tailoring window treatments and designing custom looks while not necessarily spending a lot of money. Even then, there were a few of the ladies who looked to me for guidance. It came natural to me, I suppose. And I loved helping to lead a team. We might make a rod pocket, pinch pleats, and a goblet; that's my favorite. If you look at it closely, the way it hangs on the rod—the goblet top has the most elegant silhouette, like a shapely woman dressed in a classy sheath.

When the other officers' wives came to visit, they would inevitably ask where I'd bought our nice things. Wherever we were based, no matter the city, our house was a gathering spot. And I know the ladies and their children enjoyed my hospitality. And I enjoyed that they enjoyed it.

I just think that what felt like relaxation for them was, sometimes, work for me. The headaches and blurred vision weren't things I felt comfortable sharing. And I wanted to make sure—with Frank's career—that I did all the right hosting and made the kind of connections that were necessary as an officer's wife. My husband worked awfully hard. And it wasn't easy on him. As good as he was as a leader and as an honorable military man, he was sometimes passed over. And we knew why.

I kept praying—so did Frank. Prayer has always been the centerpiece of our marriage. We never would've made it without the grace of God. Frank was easily one of the most respected men on base. And worked so very hard.

The next time my eyesight started back up with the funny business, it was nearly impossible to hide. Honestly, I couldn't see a darn thing. I didn't want the kids to be afraid. But the fact is, I was frightened myself. This wasn't normal. That much I knew. Many years later, I came to find out that although what I was going through wasn't at all normal, it was common in people with MS. And it was twice as common in African Americans than whites with the disease.

Back then, I remember my daughter Marlo was a little thing—pretty as a doll baby and a sunburst of energy. Blair and Frankie were in school all day. But Marlo was in half-day kindergarten at the time. And I don't know which one of us was more excited for her to finally get into a classroom. Oh, let me tell you—she just knew she was a big girl, joining her big brothers with somewhere to go every morning. And I loved every second of dressing her up and fixing her hair just so. After so many years of rough and tumble with my sons—and doing boy mom things—it was like I had a brand-new, precious little plaything to dote on. Baby Marlo was my sweet Hershey's kiss of girly fun.

Of course, I also enjoyed having a few hours to myself during the day. But, honestly, the hours really flew by. Seemed as though by the time I got all my children out of the house—afternoon time rudely announced itself. And then my second shift began. On this particular day, the school year had just really started. I'd say it was maybe the middle of September.

I'd picked up Marlo at noon. And at around 2:30, she and I were walking back to school to gather up the boys. Marlo was more excited than usual that day, because she'd learned to read a few words. And she couldn't wait to show Blair and Frankie how "smart I got today," in her words. Usually, all the kids came out the front door of the school at dismissal, running to their moms. I looked forward to that time, because it was a chance for me to bond with my baby girl.

Anyway, as we stood there waiting for their classes to come out—the headache came on. I knew almost instinctively what was going to happen next. I was right. Within two minutes or so, the entire schoolyard became fuzzy. And my eyes and temples were on fire. Pain shooting like daggers. I was anxious and petrified at the same time.

Before I knew what happened, Blair had run up to one hip grabbing my one hand—"Mommy! Marlo!"—and Frankie, the other. That's the way they usually bolted out of school once they spotted Marlo and me. So excited, like we hadn't seen each other in months. But on this particular day, I felt them. But I never actually saw the boys rushing toward us. In fact, I couldn't see a thing along either side of me. My peripheral vision was gone. Just gone.

As we walked home, thank God, the kids were all completely engaged in their sibling thing—one talking louder and faster than the other. Marlo never did let go of me. Baby Girl was stuck on me like Elmer's glue, which I loved. And I was never more grateful for it. She was my guide on our way from school, my Seeing Eye baby. It seemed like with each passing block my vision got dimmer and dimmer. By the time we reached the house, I couldn't see a blessed thing.

I took straight to bed. Honestly, not because I was necessarily tired. I just didn't really know what to do with myself as I waited for Frank to come home. He was working late. And I was so out of sorts. Disoriented. Dazed. Confused. Luckily, I had dinner already prepared. I told Frankie I was coming down with some kind of bug, and being the in-charge big brother was a role he always relished. He gave Blair and Marlo a few orders—which were dutifully obeyed and made sure they ate and cleaned up the dishes.

Poor Frank. When he came upstairs I collapsed in his arms. I didn't tell him about the times before. In fact, I myself hadn't fully accepted those other episodes for what they were. I was convinced they were really, really bad headaches. This was not that. I could not see. The whole situation confounded doctor after doctor.

Two weeks. It lasted two weeks.

Friends coming and going with casseroles and such. I won't say I got used to it. But I mean I felt it would be wrong for the kids to suffer. So I did all I could do to keep up with laundry. The kids never knew how bad it was. I would, well, I would make like it wasn't all that horrible. I was able to get snacks and juices together.

And when they were all done with homework, I'd say the same words I said every evening before I lost my sight: "Is that your very best?"

Even without my vision, I could see each turn a little sheepish. Then they'd go back and do it again. Their best is all I ever wanted.

Pearl of Perseverance

At the early onset of the MS, the optic nerve can swell up to the point of blindness. It was unnerving. I wanted to be done with it all. But it wasn't done with me. We kept praying. Prayer has always been the centerpiece of our marriage.
If there is anything I can do—it's see.
Part intuition. Part good sense.
Part Holy Spirit. I could always see.
And see things no one else could.

Mom in one of her favorite places—walking the runway at the Officer's Club Women's Fellowship Fashion Show.

5

LETTING GO

There is nothing I can do or say about the vacant look in my eyes—looking straight through my husband's gaze. My sunken shoulders. I know I don't look well, probably look about as bad as I feel. Every move is a chore, even eating. Sometime around 1995 when I had this depression thing hit, I had to be in the hospital. Doctors told my family, "Well if we can't get her to eat she'll be dead in about five days." This time I don't feel quite as horrible, but I am definitely not interested in food—or anything for that matter. Even as frail as I am, I feel overwhelmed by the heaviness of my limbs, as though each weighs a ton. The truth is my legs don't act like they care to belong to my body at all. They have plans all their own and had no intention of doing what I tell them to. When they are not willfully stiff and heavy as concrete bricks, they are blazing like a white-hot wildfire.

So it seems only sensible to lie there. In bed. All day. For weeks. For months. Maybe years. Right now, I don't know.

My body no longer takes me where I want to go. Downstairs? Well, that trip may as well be miles long. The staircase in this big old house winds down to the lower level. If you picture a grand colonial house, this is it. Well, this *is* Petersburg, Virginia—the heart of the colonial tradition. Days like today, the house feels massive and tiny at the same time: too big to maneuver, yet—because of my physical limitations—tiny, almost as though the walls are closing in around me. I just cannot make it down the steps. And, no—for God's sake—I don't want help. I'm sick and tired of help. No matter how well meaning. And Lord knows I realize that it all comes from a place of love. But how many times can a person lean on to and be held up by another person's strength before they begin to feel powerless? I'm sick and tired. And at this point, *I'm sick and tired of being sick and tired.*

No one can possibly understand what this is like. I hear them mumbling to one another, saying, "She's depressed again," as though I'm not here. They think, I suppose, I'm really not here—that my entire being is as far off as my blank stares—or that I hear maybe, but somehow I don't understand the words coming out of their mouths. Or the way they keep looking at me from the crack in the doorway. Wondering if I'm going to try to swallow a handful of pills again. I know that ever since the day last year, when I tried to leap out of the speeding car, Frank and the children haven't looked at me the same.

It's as though I am one of those delicate porcelain figurines on the downstairs mantel—I might break apart into a hundred pieces, sharp pieces, though, that could cut their fingers or pierce their hearts. Past episodes, if that's what we're calling this, have hurt them. I own it: My words have been harsh, my patience bare. And I've been unpleasant to be around. Can't really say how long it's been since I ventured out of my bedroom. There is a balcony to the right of the bedside table. I like to gaze out on to it, overlooking the garden.

Where does the time go? Now that I think about it, I have watched at least a couple of seasons pass from my bed. This morning Frank was in a sweater. And I remember days when the balcony was covered with snow. Frank would just stand by the bed a while and breathe. This disease has been hard on him, too. I overhear him, voice dripping with sadness, saying to Frankie: "I just want my wife back."

I feel bad about Frankie's wedding day. My firstborn

takes a wife and I couldn't even show up in good spirits. I was truly happy and excited for my son's future. Love is all that matters in this life. He and his lovely wife stood before God. And it seems I just couldn't quite get it together; everything and everyone irritated me. Hindsight is twenty-twenty. Probably I should've tried to explain how bad my body was attacking me. The early part of the week hadn't been so bad. My body was numb and sore, like I'd gone a few rounds with Mike Tyson. But that wasn't too, too awful—those feelings were an everyday thing. But as we prepared for the rehearsal dinner my skin was burning as though thousands of tiny needles were stabbing me from head to toe.

I know now that MS beats up on the body's nerves, and even the nerve lining around them within the central nervous system. Those damaged nerve fibers can cause almost everything to go haywire, and my symptoms are things like blurred vision, mobility issues—when and if I can get around, I feel unsteady, like I'll lose my balance, tremors, and severe pain. There are two main kinds of MS pain: neuropathic pain and also musculoskeletal pain.

All of the big words simply mean the signals between my central nervous system and the rest of my body are all a tangled mess. My spinal cord is deteriorating. Not every person with MS gets every symptom. Some people get a few at a time. And they come in waves. Now for me, from what I can tell—once I get almost accustomed to one set of ailments, here come a half dozen new ones.

My body, for example, hurts all the time. But get this, the doctors say MS is not entirely the cause. The disease makes your muscles weak. Okay? Just to give you an idea, a year or so ago I started to notice my one foot would get numb; it didn't want to hold my weight. It wasn't painful, just kind of limp and useless. So I dragged it. I'd take a step with my right foot, drag the left—over and over; just step and repeat. I mean, it got me where I needed to go! What I learned later is that favoring that side had put undue pressure on my hip and back. That's where the muscle pain usually comes from with MS—not the disease itself so much, but what most people do to compensate for the ill effects of the disease. Ain't that a kick in the head!

The skin burning, stinging, and itchy-crawly feeling is chronic—it pretty much never goes away. Sometimes it's only horribly aggravating: Imagine having a picnic, a few ants show up and crawl up your arm, then they call all their friends and cover your entire body. It may not hurt but it's maddening. Know what I'm saying? Some of the medicines help, but only a little. Other times it's insufferable, keeps me up at night, and makes me swear I'm losing my mind—as though something, or someone, is on the inside of my body, under my skin fighting to get out, almost drilling their way out.

I can just be going about my business, dealing with the itchy-crawly tingling when what's called an MS relapse will come calling. That means one of two things: I might get an entirely new thing pop up or the other possibility is that whatever I'm dealing with in the moment suddenly gets worse. It goes from a nuisance to crushing pain. There's this one thing I get now and again that's especially bad. It's agonizing but also just very scary because it seems to come out of nowhere.

There's even a special name for it: the MS hug. But don't let that cute name fool you. The "hug" is more like a gripping spasm that takes hold right between my ribs. It can last a few minutes, or an hour or two. And it can come and go. The thing is, when the hug decides to visit, it doesn't care what your other symptoms are up to. Sometimes I am already entertaining the numbness and weakness in my muscles, and the tingling might escalate to what feels like an electric shock—then the hug comes on top of all that. It's more than I can take sometimes.

And I really have no choice. I shut down for a spell. It's not as though I can explain any of this to Frank and the kids. As far as they're concerned, I'm right up there with Superwoman. Maybe some of that is my own doing. I know they hate seeing me like this. Who hates it more than I do?

Treating me like a wayward child at times. Talking all slow, tiptoeing around. Probably they're scared I'm working on some other plan to take myself away from here to take my life. What they don't understand is I don't have the strength to plan anything. When I tried to get out of the moving car, it was a split-second decision. I hated the idea of going to the doctor—again. I'd soiled the outfit I was wearing—literally smelling myself, and I just got so damned angry I had to do something right then and there. I was awfully sorry to frighten them so. But I was also awfully sorry they managed to stop me.

For now, I'm going to simply lie here. Still. Quiet. I don't know how long I've been lying here and I don't want to know. There is nothing I can do or say. On my bedside table, all the medicines and ointments and whatnot seem a bit silly. What good are they if after all this time, I can't get down the steps of my own house?

"What's wrong?" they keep asking. Just because I'm not talking, it doesn't mean I can't hear. I have four grown children—and now they've got children of their own. Why are they so obsessed with why I'm still in the bed? How many times are Frank and the children going to whisper all around me? It's annoying, all the constant chatter and head scratching. Can't I just lie down?

I suppose I get it. They're worried. Confused. Frightened. Well, guess what? So am I.

When my doctor visits come around, the answers—if you can call them that—are always the same:

"MS is different for everyone."

"Symptoms vary, sometimes flare-ups fluctuate from day to day."

"We don't know exactly what causes MS."

"You can have a long period of remission—or you may not."

"MS can progress slowly—though for some people, it progresses quickly."

"There is still much to be studied about MS."

Sometimes I wanna scream—tell Frank and the kids: "If doctors can't explain this madness, how can I?" I'm not my old self, that's for sure. Can't say I feel sick exactly. At least, not in the way anyone would understand. And I don't have the energy to entertain any conversation around the matter.

Frank wants to know about this month's bills. Have I paid them? Folks are wondering about the year's church picnic. Did I order enough balloons for the children? Maybe I oughta get another hundred or so. Last year, there weren't enough. Soon, I'll need to start planning the gospel Christmas pageant, and then all of the holiday parties we do at the house. December will be busy as usual. This year, I really want to outdo myself; I'll definitely need more lights. I was so frustrated when the one string across the banister blew out. Thankfully, they didn't go dark till News Year's Eve, but it still nearly ruined the "winter wonderland" look I was going for. And I want dozens of Christmas trees all over the house!

Oh, goodness, and then we'll have the annual Amway party—I can't even begin to think about all the Amway business that needs tending to. I really should tidy things up in the product room. And I'm behind on my "time to reorder" notes I send to my best customers. If they miss out on the Nutrilite supplements, the shipments might get backlogged. What's nice is there's new packaging that will roll out in the next few months. You can get the "women's pack" and then add a fiber or iron folic at a really great value. It's a lot—let me tell you.

But right now, I've had enough of doing, and doing. Everyone wants something, needs something. I just need to press pause for once. Guess I've brought this on myself—all the expectations. I have no regrets. I've loved taking care of my house, my husband, my family, the church, the business, friends, too. Always. In my heart, I know it's what I was born to do.

When MS was first mentioned by a specialist I saw in the 1990s, I was relieved in a way to have a possible explanation—finally. But did she ever ask a lot of silly questions! *Do you lead a stressful life?* I looked at her for a moment. "Well, of course," I thought. "Is there a wife and mother whose life is not filled with stress? *Can you tell me about your "stress-management" techniques?* I told her I pray to my Heavenly Father, without ceasing. Then *she* was the one confused. Ha! Finally, I'd stumped *her*. How do you like that?

People talk about stress as though I've chosen it—told it to come in and take a seat. I didn't invite stress into my life. And, truth be told, I don't think I even knew stress was a big part of my life. I've always had a lot on me—so has every other woman I know. I *wanted* to work hard to be a good mother and a good wife to Frank. I guess I was too busy for all those years—packing, unpacking, moving wherever the army told us to: Germany, Michigan, Colorado, Virginia, Washington State—wherever Frank was stationed we considered "home." And I would make sure it felt like home. With each move, I sewed new drapes and decorated—the quarters were pretty drab, functional, but usually a bit bleak. And I wanted Frank and the kids to be comfortable.

I thought if I made everything look warm and elegant, the transition would be smoother. And, of course, every two years we pick up stakes and do it again. I needed to get the children into school; find all the activities in a given city to help them continue doing the things they enjoyed—sports, art, music; manage PTA duties; search for a church home; and, of course, stay on top of all the scheduling. And, naturally, I had to set about making new friends. Easy-peasy for me. I love meeting new people, learning, laughing, and hosting. But there was some work involved—if nothing else to make sure I found the "right" social set. At that time, there was no diversity in the ranks of army officers—so we're talking about all white women, for the most part. That didn't bother me any. All I knew was that I wanted to make Frank's life as smooth as possible. He needed a wife who could blend in socially with his peers.

Oh, how he brags about the way I got on with the other officers' wives, how I was one of his biggest cheerleaders and strongest assets. All true. I knew the kind of scrutiny he was under. The armed forces had really been desegregated for only a short time. There were people looking for reasons to exclude him—to cast doubt on his qualifications. We know, but it bears repeating the old saying: a Black person has to be twice as good to get half as much as the whites.

We knew we were in a fishbowl of sorts. Baby, we had to be *on* at all times. Now quite naturally, he was a man of substance. But it helped that I had style, to tell the truth. I knew it was important that I make him look good. Not just on the surface. Heck, anyone can wear nice clothes. There is an elegance and grace that plays a role. By that I mean getting on with people, sharing a good story—just engaging with people in a way that would make us not only stand out, but also fit in at the same time. Wives have a great deal of influence over their husbands, you know. Social events were very important, never as frivolous as you might think.

See as women, we tend to bond over beautiful things. Sure I could've thrown some of anything together and

I would've looked fine. That's what most of the wives did. I went the extra mile. I usually opted to wear elegant Empire-waist dresses—something very Jackie Kennedy–like. That's my MO, so to speak. I liked to wear pastels most times, robin's-egg blue maybe, because, baby, that's the kind of color that is outta sight against a brown complexion like mine. Listen, I don't make the rules. It's the truth. Why, all the wives would compliment my outfit, of course. And, before you knew it, we're exchanging numbers and making plans to get our children together.

There was a lot riding on those kinds of occasions. I knew that in order for Frank's career to continue rising, I had to be an asset to him. He often told me stories about the unlucky servicemen with wives who simply weren't cut out for army life. Maybe they were withdrawn or nervous or overwhelmed—there are all kinds of reasons why the whole thing might not suit a woman. The way I look at it, I had to be ready to just kind of roll with the punches. Was it difficult at times? You bet.

But remember, at the end of the day, I'm still a wife and mother—no matter what. So it's up to me to keep everyone happy and everything running smoothly. My friends back home had the same responsibilities. But then, of course, they had the benefit of support: family who might take the kids off your hands for a few hours; a church home, where you have a shared history; longtime neighbors; or even a hairdresser you might share beauty secrets with.

Speaking of hairdressers, I found a work-around pretty quickly. I mean there was no way any of the on-base beauty parlors would know a press-and-curl if it slapped them in the face! I had just about every kind of wig you could imagine. It was a quick fix. And I knew how to style them, with some of my own hair blended, to make each one look as natural as possible. I look back on those days, and I sometimes wonder how I managed to *be all* the things *all* the time—and look good doing it. Praise God. After a while it became second nature. In a million years, I never saw the life I find myself living now. I don't do well with the nothingness of it all. Know what I mean? It's hard to explain. Yesterday was the same as today. Tomorrow and the next day will be like reruns of the same show. It's maddening. Nothing but the blood of Jesus can stop this sorry loop. For all the prodding and poking. All the pills and potions. What now? That's what I keep wondering.

What I do know is, if this is what life is going to be—then *this* is no kind of life that's worth living. And I don't really want to be here anymore. I mean, for what? Blair tells me "a lot of famous people have MS, Mom." He even had me all the way out to LA—where he lives—and took me to the doctors who treat Annette Funicello and the talk show guy Montel Williams. We had appointments with all the fanciest of MDs. And they had lots to say about experimental this and experimental that. There are trials here and trials there. Diets, and certain foods I should eat. And—of course—many foods I should cut back on, including sugar.

Anyone who knows me will tell you how much I enjoy my Butterfinger candies and Lorna Doone shortbread cookies. From the time I was a little girl, they have always been my favorites. And I usually keep the cupboards well stocked with my goodies. The experts in this disease say that studies show sugar makes people with MS even more fatigued, which is pretty devastating to learn. Because that's probably the hardest part of living this MS life.

And the real kicker is that I'm tired for no good reason—the kind of tired I feel is worse than any exhaustion I've ever felt. And nobody gets it. You can say to people all day long, "Oh, I'm tired today." And they think they know what you mean. Heck, everyone has been tired, right? Everyone knows what that's like. At the end of a long day, you figure—oh, I feel fatigued; I've gone to work; I've taken care of the children; cooked dinner or whatever—tiredness will set in.

But, baby, this is no regular tired. That's what I'm trying to say. It's like the worst, most extreme jet lag ever—where your body is three times its normal weight and quicksand is pulling you under. So heavy I can barely move—definitely can't concentrate. My brain is like soup. It may sound crazy to say, but the tired feeling from this disease might just be worse than the pain. At least the pain can ebb and flow at times. This hit-by-a-Mack-truck kind of fatigue doesn't budge. And all the doctors say is: *Well, roughly 85 percent of MS patients get that.* They give you statistics all the time. No real answers.

The other information I get from doctors and the pamphlets in their offices? Advice that makes no sense. They'll say, *conserve your energy*. And I'm thinking, "What energy?" I read about all these tips for good "sleep hygiene." Now, a medical doctor should know good and well that going to bed at the same time every night is not going to help a person sleep through pain. Or once, very early on, one of them suggested getting groceries delivered. I mean, that's a very expensive way to shop. I read an entire brochure filled with the idea of breaking down big tasks into smaller, more manageable tasks. Obviously if I could think more clearly, like I did years ago, I'd have done that. The problem is my mind hasn't wanted to work with me in ages. Between menopause and MS, I can't even remember the last time I was able to really plan without this foggy brain of mine.

Yes, some of the medicines are supposed to help. The problem with that is that some of the other side effects of MS keep the drugs from helping much. I'm more prone to urinary tract and other bacterial infections, and they make you feel tired. MS messes up my thyroid and iron levels, and that causes fatigue. The restless leg syndrome I get every so often drains my energy. See where I'm going? The drugs are like a drip in a bucket filled with water.

I often wake up tired. Or feel tired after barely putting out any energy—like after trying to send a text message. Seriously. Some days it can feel like I've got to use all the strength in my body and in my brain to write a note. And I hate it. You know why? Sloth is a mortal sin—that's what I was raised to believe. Laziness has no place in the character of a Christ follower. Heaven is not promised to Christians who prove to be lazy. Think about the Parable of the Talents, right? The servant with five talents went out and gained five more. The servant with two talents doubled the value he was given. We know that the third did nothing with his talent—just hid it in the ground. Shameful.

I know that God knows my heart. I pray on it. And I try hard to be patient, to make some sense of the constant stillness. But it just doesn't sit well in my spirit. I know, in my head, that it's the cruelty of disease draining me. But it is still very troubling. The energy that has been robbed from me, even knowing what I know about MS, makes me feel like a failure—like I'm turning into a lazy person all of a sudden. It's completely against my nature to be sitting up doing next to nothing. What can come of that? I try to fight it most days. I really do. But it's like I'm damned if I do and damned if I don't. Because you know what happens when I put up a good, strong fight? You guessed it—I'm even more tired. I feel like giving up. I can't win. The whole thing is a vicious cycle.

The monotony of today feels a lot like yesterday, last week, and last month; time tends to blend together. But there is a bit of hullabaloo stirring about the house. Blair is flying in from LA. We always get very excited to have him home, even for a short visit. Seems not that long ago that news of him taking a short break from filming a series or movie would get me in planning mode right off. I'd be on my way to the grocery store right now under normal circumstances, getting all the ingredients for his favorite foods—baking a *lot*, because let me tell you, that boy inherited my sweet tooth!

But nothing has been normal for quite some time. I'm pretty sure somebody, Marlo maybe, sent word and told Blair to come see about me. He's a good egg. All my children are wonderful people. I am so blessed. Each one has their own special gifts: Of course, Blair was bitten by the acting bug and has found great success. Frank Jr. is a profoundly talented visual artist, several of his paintings hang on these walls. Marlo, like me, nurtures her creative genius on the sidelines while she raises her three boys and goes above and beyond to be the best wife, mother, and daughter she can possibly be. Mellisa, the baby, is happier than I've seen her in years, now that she is living her passion as a chef.

God has been very good to me. Nothing but gratitude fills my heart when I think about His grace. My family has always been my everything, and to have been on this earth long enough to see them thrive is such a joy. They will be fine without me.

From my bed I can see the hallway. The long corridor bridges over the foyer on the lower level of the house. It's one of the reasons I fell in love with this home years ago. Once Frank retired and we prepared to settle into civilian life, I knew I wanted a double-height entry foyer and a grand staircase—something reminiscent of a scene out of a Spencer Tracy–Katharine Hepburn movie like *Guess Who's Coming to Dinner.* All of the classic films had this kind of stairway. When I saw it, I knew this was the house for us—perfect for prom photos, weddings, and the like. And it has given us so many love-filled years, fond memories, and—oh, goodness—tons of laughter.

Much of the colorway on the first level came to me from the idea of Colonial Williamsburg's traditional American style. This is Virginia, after all. The walls are painted a rich, saturated shade of Chesapeake blue with Capitol white trim. It's definitely stately and sophisticated, especially in the 1980s, when I first decorated. Lots of people were doing an inelegant country cottage-y mix of color that was lovely in a way, but flat—with no dimension. My ideas—the drapes, which I made, of course, the furnishings, the walls—have stood the test of time.

I can see the top of the banister right outside my bedroom door. I've had plenty of time as I lie here to size it up. And it is really not as tall as one might think. I've never been very athletic, but before the throes of MS, most would probably describe me as fairly big-boned. I definitely come from sturdy stock. Back in the day, I'd fill out a size 14 dress handily. I'm feeling like I can take that banister. "The thud of my brittle body hitting that foyer should be enough to take me out of here," I think. I am ready—been ready—to be with the Lord.

One thing about me: When I set my mind on something, you can believe it's as good as done.

Pearl of Letting Go

My body no longer moves with me, only against me. The pain, fatigue, blank stares—they've stolen who I was. I've lived for others, given everything, even as MS quietly took more and more. Now, I lie still. Tired. Done performing. Done pretending. Letting go means releasing guilt, the need to explain, the weight of expectations. Maybe even the need to stay. I've made a beautiful life. Loved well. Raised strong children. Now I long for rest—true rest. If God is calling me home, I'm ready.

Mom and me at the opening night of A Streetcar Named Desire on Broadway, April 22, 2012, at the Copacabana Club after party.

6

SUCCESS

It's strange to my way of thinking. But do you know, there are people in this world who wait their whole lives to "make it"? Whatever that means. After all, I suppose to each of us it's a little something different. Some folks are hoping their luck will change. Searching for a pot of gold, they chase rainbow after rainbow. Or they're looking for that "big break." Crossing their fingers, in fact, that somehow all the stars will align.

That's a fool's gambit.

There is this very unique quality in Frank—and, in a way, we both share the belief—that holds to the theory that you are as successful as your mind can hold. In other words, you choose your dream and then you will yourself to do what you have to do. It's funny in a way. Because nowadays, we have all these books in the market on this very thing. And important people like Oprah Winfrey and others are devotees. But Frank and I have always lived by the idea that you—each of us, really—create your own destiny. The highbrow name for the very simple principle is probably best known as "the law of attraction."

Frank would say that once you tell your mind what you've already decided in your heart, you then create a set of habits. And you live that out. Once you do, other events and thoughts and experiences will naturally fall in line. And before you know it, one step has led to another and another and another.

Now I am a strong believer—and so is Frank. Of course, there is no such thing as pure will or luck and you can't simply tell yourself a thing and wiggle your nose like *Bewitched*. Faith without works is dead. But if I know anything about life, it's that when you adjust the way you think, you can change the way you feel. And more than half of what you achieve is based on how able, how prepared you are, to achieve it.

Henry Ford said it best: "Whether you think you can or you think you can't—you're right." And I refuse to subscribe to a small or limited system of belief. Look at all this goodness God put on the earth. Why? For His children, of course!

To anyone who knows—I mean, really knows—me, this won't necessarily be surprising. But I'll share a story to show just how much stock Frank and I put into the mindset I'm talking about.

Frank has his command out of Fort Carson; that's situated near Colorado Springs, okay? Well, we were really taken with the beauty of that part of the country: the mountains, the vistas, the foothills of the Rockies. It's probably the most naturally spectacular place Frank and I had ever seen. And what we wanted, more than anything, was a ranch. That's right. These two northerners didn't bat an eye at the idea of living on a huge expanse of ranchland. We talked about it and talked about it, told anybody who'd listen that this was our intent. At this point and time, we figured it would make a wonderful place to live, once Frank had retired. And retirement wasn't too, too far out. We did some looking, but we didn't find a property that seemed to fit our needs.

Then, just as Frank had gotten another assignment, this time at the Pentagon—which meant moving close to Washington—we got a call from friends who said: "There's this amazing ranch for sale. It's seven hundred and twenty beautiful acres. You gotta come and take a look. It's just what you've been dreaming of."

Well, all we could think was, *"Here we are about to move to Washington, so the timing isn't great."* But we decided to take a look anyway. And you know what? It was perfect. We absolutely fell in love—this ranch was exactly what we wanted. So we put in an offer.

You know, love makes you do all kinds of things. And this here was one of those moments when we knew we needed to just step out on faith. Frank had more than I did in this particular case. He just knew we'd be able to make it work. We put all of the paperwork into the purchase of this huge ranch at the same time that we were in the process of moving to a new city almost one thousand seven hundred miles away. And I promise you, we had no idea where the money was coming from. Not only did we not know where the money would come from, but we also weren't really worried.

We moved to Alexandria, Virginia, that summer; and by the fall, we received a phone call that would change our lives forever, in a good way. Between the time we left Colorado and the holidays, we discovered Amway.

Even before I met him, my husband had just breathed confidence and integrity. So it shouldn't have been surprising when a childhood friend of his contacted us with so much excitement and joy it was simply contagious. His childhood classmate from Steubenville, Ohio, Eileen Thompson, is someone he always kept in close contact with—she and her husband, Mike, were great friends to us. They sent us postcards, which was common back in those days, all the time—whether it was from their travels or their home in Newport News. And when I think back, they'd mentioned something about a new venture in one of their cards a year or so prior. But we were preoccupied. In their annual holiday card, Eileen had written: "We've gone into business!"

We couldn't imagine what kind of business they were into and didn't pay a whole lot of attention. But as we were starting to settle into Alexandria, the four of us began to get really excited that we'd be in the same state—there is only a two-hour-or-so drive from Alexandria to Newport News. I guess it was around the latter part of the summer when we called to catch up, and Mike got on the phone. Now, what you need to know is, Mike is a quiet fellow—very subdued. Eileen was a Chatty Cathy and great fun. Mike was the exact opposite.

So, after I'd spoken to Eileen for a while Frank got on the phone with Mike. And when he hung up he turned to me and said: "You won't believe it, but Mike has completely changed. I don't think he's ever been so excited. He said this business is like nothing he's ever done before."

At first, I was a little worried—thought something must be wrong. For Mike that was already more than I'd ever heard him express. I'm telling you, this man was so quiet, at times I'd tell Frank: "I really don't wanna drive down to see them sometimes. You and Eileen are sure to get to talking about all the fun you had as kids—which is fine. But then Mike and I will be staring at the floor, because every attempt I make at conversation is met with a one-word answer."

This conversation, on the other hand, had Frank so animated. He was almost giddy. He said Eileen and Mike were coming up to see us, to take us through "The Plan." I thought to myself, "The what?" But his energy was contagious, it almost didn't matter. They arrived a couple of weeks later, and we all sat around the kitchen table, and Eileen was convinced that we had the work ethic, personalities, and contacts to be successful. I hadn't known anything about Amway before that night at the table, but direct sales seemed like a natural fit for Frank and me. I'd never heard of multilevel marketing. But we both love people—meeting people, mentoring people— and the products are very much in line with my lifestyle. I love products that make my life better. The cleaning products are natural. So to me that means taking better care of my home and family. Health and well-being are areas I've always gravitated toward: vitamins, supplements, soaps. It all fits me. In many ways it's not even "work" because I'm championing things I really believe in.

And Amway's principles truly resonate with Frank and me. He has served his country with honor. I respect a brand that focuses on love of country and American values. Like the name says, Amway is all about the American way: freedom, family, hope, and reward. Who wouldn't love to be part of something like this? We're all in it together—when Frank and I bring someone in, their value adds to our value. We're a family really.

The core values are part and parcel of the way Frank and I live our lives. From my perspective, when you learn about the values behind the business it's a no-brainer:

PARTNERSHIP—Amway is based on the common good, you see. The company's success comes directly from the success of people who start their own business and sell the products.

INTEGRITY—We're bound by a code of sorts, to work together and do what's right, not just what works. I read about it and let it all sink in: PERSONAL WORTH—ACHIEVEMENT—PERSONAL RESPONSIBILITY—FREE ENTERPRISE.

Naturally, we let our guests, Mike and Eileen, explain the business and go through all the things we would need to consider. But about halfway through The Plan, our eyes met. And Frank knew what I was thinking, and I knew what he was thinking: "This is it! Here's how we will pay for the ranch in Colorado." God will always make a way—especially when we, as mere mortals, see no way.

We were in. I don't even know that we talked that much about the *how* of it all. Not that we thought it would be easy. No one hands you anything in life. Frank had his job at the Pentagon, and we knew that he couldn't mix Amway with his job at the Pentagon. It was just something we almost immediately understood. So we decided very early that I'd handle the more visible parts of the business initially. I just said, "I'm going into this carrying my part—period." Because I knew what was at stake.

So I started making contacts—started the very next day in fact. I was thrilled, because it meant a way to make some terrific money. I got on the phone all of the next day. And I went through eighteen couples in the blink of an eye—fourteen of them accepted, and they all agreed to come by the house. Now you know why they came? Because I was so excited about this business. They just couldn't imagine what would have turned me on like that.

I have loved our Amway business. In fact, it feels as though I was born to it. From the time I was a young girl in Buffalo, I saw myself running a business. It's as if it was all preordained. In every city where Frank had been stationed, I began making contacts. The challenge of it all was very exhilarating and chaotic at the same time. I still had to juggle mothering, and PTA, and church choir, *and* my duties as an officer's wife. Any one of those alone could be a lot. To me, each and every role gave me an opportunity to make Amway connections. There was literally no encounter I didn't use as an opening—when the boys, both Blair and Frankie, played football or ran track or joined the swim team, those parents were potential customers and partners. I found it so easy to talk about because I was all in—a genuine believer in the great opportunity Amway offered.

At all times, even when I was tired, my eyes were on the prize. Eileen and Mike fired us up. And I could very quickly see that the five or six people you meet who get The Plan easily leads to twenty more. It worked like this. I mean, the money was remarkably simple to make. We were distributors. Then, I'd make contact with potentials—pretty much on a regular basis. Once I had a good-size group of people interested, I'd invite them over to the house. The goal was to show The Plan as often as possible—the more you show, the greater your potential for success. Frank would go to work and perform all of his duties at the Pentagon. Then he'd come home, and I'd already have everything organized. Of course we'd socialize a bit. Then, Frank would take over with the big white easel. He'd map out everything in black and white: the products, the sales plan, who you'd work with, the teamwork concept, the revenue stream, and the way it all laddered up to success. Then those who joined became part of our network. Frank and I would be their sponsors, you see.

They'd go out and do their own selling and build their own networks, and all of that lived under Frank and me. People would call in and report their sales. That way I could make sure we had the inventory. Maybe I'd need to drive to the warehouse. The goal was to keep the product room we maintained at the house well stocked with all of the most popular items. Folks would come to the house, load up their cars with their customers' orders filled. And the way any multilevel marketing program works, that business that they have, those sales, are also ours.

I'm not exaggerating when I say it took off like a rocket! We amassed a very large and very successful organization in no time. Amway was business but it was also fun, because these were all people we viewed as family.

We were able to share the gift of entrepreneurship with those we care about—literally sharing the wealth. Who doesn't want greater financial independence? And as a married couple, how could you turn down a chance to really invest in and build something together with your husband or wife? The business definitely brought relationships closer together. I know it did ours.

The most meaningful thing about the business was that Frank and I were a team; it was an extension of our lifelong partnership. His time was limited, of course. I was, by default, more the nuts-and-bolts operations-end of the business. Frank was military and had his full-time job. And we had to be very discreet, because his boss lived on our same block in Arlington! Looking back, it was a hilarious adventure at times.

All the kids helped out. In each of the houses we moved to, we always had a "product room" where we kept Amway inventory. And the kids would help ship out the soaps, vitamins, and such. Blair was really intrigued by the business. When we moved to Michigan, in fact, he decided as a middle schooler that he wanted to get involved.

One of his teachers at the time, Mr. Sage, was Blair's first success. We practiced a little bit—what he might say—how he'd broach the subject. Mr. Sage was this long-haired gentleman, unassuming, cool; he was pretty popular with the kids. Well, one day Blair walked up to him after class, and with his thirteen-to-fourteen-year-old self said: "Mr. Sage, would you be interested in making an extra thousand dollars a month?"

And, to his great surprise, Mr. Sage was curious. He didn't brush Blair off as a kid with no clue about what he was saying. All Blair could say in response was, "Come over to our house. My parents can explain everything." Do you know the Sages went on to become some of our strongest sellers?

With the network we built, it wasn't long before our living room just couldn't accommodate the crowds we would draw. Frank and I had to start hosting in meeting spaces and hotels. We rose all the way up to the Emerald level, and we were speaking at Amway conferences to groups in the hundreds, and sometimes the thousands. It was absolutely phenomenal. Boggles the mind. Even to this day, Amway is still making revenue for Frank and me!

We weren't naive. We were fully aware of the naysayers. We just kind of tuned them out. Many people believed what we were doing with Amway—what legions of people were doing—was too good to be true. They didn't understand how it was possible for the business model to work as famously as it does. But that's because those of us who really believed in the business were practically religious about it. We loved it and we wanted to spread the word. People will always be eager to find some negativity if they can. What they didn't see was the hard work that was behind the scenes. When you enjoy what you do, sometimes you don't even think about the tough times. You don't complain because the fruits of your labor are so evident.

Friends would occasionally call Frank and just want to find out, "Hey, are you still in that Amway thing?" "Hey, does that thing really work?" And they were really, really trying to find out once the success of our business was so obvious. "Does it work?" they'd ask. It's funny, thinking back. A part of me wanted to say, "Well, what does it look like? Can't you see that it works?" But you keep the door open for your friends; you don't close it—keep it open. One day they may see it for what it is, but don't wait and don't worry about it.

Pearl of Success

Once you tell your mind what you've already decided in your heart, you then create a set of habits. And before you know it, one step has led to another and another and another. When you adjust the way you think, you can change the way you feel. And more than half of what you achieve is based on how able, how prepared you are to achieve it.

Mom and Dad's wedding day,
April 23, 1960, Buffalo, New York.

7

LEADERSHIP

There are days I put my wheelchair in the living room and gaze out the window. As the gospel song says: "As I look back over my life and think things over, I can truly say that I've been blessed."

Indeed.

We settled here in Petersburg, Virginia, just before Frank retired from the US Army in the early 1980s. After so many years of moving from base to base, I had an almost storybook vision of our permanent home. This block fits that vision perfectly. It's a pretty and quiet street—idyllic, really.

But I marvel at how, in the still of the morning, one

activity is constant: those Amazon delivery vans. The pandemic has all of us shut in. And, of course, the trucks don't always stop at my neighbors, but it seems like they are always coming up the street or going down the street—whizzing through all day and every day. What are people buying and in need of in such a hurry? Only heaven knows.

I do know that as simple as it may look from sitting here in the window—the products, the delivery, the customer service—none of it just happens. Success in business is like success in life: thousands of small, sometimes seemingly insignificant steps.

Unlike my husband, I never went to college. I don't have the kind of formal education that some people in business use to structure their enterprise. But that's never stopped me because I know in my heart that at the center of business growth is people. Plain and simple. I mean if you don't have great people alongside you, folks you can nurture and coach—who have the same vision you have and value the connection you share—then who are you actually leading? Sure, I handled the Amway bookkeeping and did the reconciling, but I never lost sight of the fact that those numbers—no matter how many zeroes—don't amount to a hill of beans if you're not focused on lifting up people.

Just the thought of those days brings a smile to my face. As these Amazon trucks checker the block, they take me back to a time in my life when Frank and I were actively building our own business. I probably lived and breathed Amway in those days. Selling and moving products were important aspects of the business. It was a major production. And the whir of all of it seemed constant. Let me tell you, it was no walk in the park. But I can't recall ever dreading or complaining about the organized chaos. And that's because of the relationships we had. I feel so blessed that the people who came into our lives through Amway became our closest friends. They were the cherry on top of a very delicious cake. Over the years they were the couples we socialized with, traveled with, and just did life with.

So many wonderful memories.

Where did human connection end and business begin? That's just it. That's the joy. Amway helped form this perfect circle where work was your fun and fun was your work. Because Frank and I love pouring into people, sharing our faith, and growing, I believe God brought those same kinds of folks into our lives.

When we met Moses and Audrey, we had a very strong feeling. We really clicked. And sure enough, we sponsored them. Then through them, we met Julius and Veronica. They sponsored Vernon and Patricia. And that's how we met Terry and Irene—and ultimately Odell and Bobby became part of our organization.

Now when I say you barely see a separation between

business, life, family, and friends, here's what I mean: outside of Amway, we would travel to different parenting conferences. At the time, ADHD and other learning styles were being discovered and talked about, and we wanted to learn more. When Blair was cast in his first film—*Krush Groove*—about twenty of us piled into a theater in Northern Virginia to watch it together. This was back when I'd started the Blair Underwood Booster Club. I'd call on my friends, then they'd call their friends whenever Blair had a movie or TV role. When Frank Jr. was taking off as a fine artist, all our friends supported his work; he's so talented. Marlo babysat for countless couples. And when Mellisa started cooking, everyone supported that, too.

    I tell you, between order taking and product shipping, we'd be just chatting it up and laughing. Most of us were parents. And the moms and I shared a special bond. We were constantly sharing advice and trading stories. Oh, nothing was off-limits. We had a time talking about style, children, husbands—and what I liked to call "taking care of home." I really tickled the ladies with that, because it's something I live by. As wives, we can forget our husbands—not intentionally, of course. And it's important to understand that you're not doing enough if you just cook, clean, and take care of the children. Men have *needs*, and when a man becomes a husband those needs don't go away. Men are not like us. You've gotta build them up emotionally, satisfy them physically, keep yourself up, and look like you're still dating. I would tell the ladies: "Stop what you're doing about an hour before your husband is due home from work, and get yourself together—do your hair, freshen your makeup, put on a flattering outfit. Because just because you're married to him doesn't mean you've got him!" The ladies would fall out laughing, but I speak the truth. It's important. And it's all connected to success. Your partnership with your husband in life and in business needs to be strong and as healthy as can be. It takes work, and wives need to understand that. You can easily fall into thinking, "Oh, I'm so busy with the children and the PTA and groceries." And it's true, but you can never forget your relationship with your husband is the foundation of it all. Presentation matters. Look your best, most beautiful self every day, and make sure good loving is a priority.

Besides, when you're surrounded by these fabulous products—creams that make your skin soft and youthful, shampoos that get your hair smelling nice—it only makes sense to take advantage of all the lovely ways to spark the senses. I was a walking, breathing billboard for Amway. And I encouraged my sellers to be the same. Remember that hilarious commercial? I forget what the ad was even selling. I think some kind of organic shampoo. But the woman standing in the middle of the grocery store starts to wash her hair. And the smell is so good, the experience so exciting, and she's panting and shouting, "Yes! Yes!" And Dr. Ruth, the famous sex expert, says: "If you think that's good, try the body wash."

Heck, I like to think of Amway independent business owners like myself as the influencers and Amazons of our day. Nearly four hundred products. Everything you might imagine—nutrition, beauty, personal health, fitness, cleaning, and home. You name it. Sometimes people aren't fully aware that they're using an Amway product, because there are so many different brands under the umbrella.

But if you sold Amway—especially when the company went through the explosive growth of the 1980s—you knew it. Your orders were bursting. And you were hustling to fulfill them.

These were the days before cell phones, apps, online shopping, and next-day delivery. I mean how is that even possible? Think about it. Folks go on their computers. An item they fancy moves to their "shopping cart" and then—poof! A click here, a click there. They go about their day, wake up, enjoy a cup of coffee, and like magic there's the item—set right on their porch. They never had to leave the house—didn't even have to shower or brush their teeth if they didn't feel like it.

I know we all take it for granted. But sometimes I stop and think, and I marvel, really, at the way the world has changed. The way my life has changed. This wheelchair pretty much turned life upside down.

Once upon a time my very existence was nearly consumed by order-taking, product-packing, and package-shipping. I knew the UPS driver by name. We were colleagues in a way, work buddies. Although Frank was no longer deployed every two years, he still held down demanding jobs. He was at the Pentagon, where he directed the army's Race Relations and Equal Opportunities Program. And later he was Professor of Military Service at Virginia State University.

I handled much of the day-to-day business operations while he was at the office. I was on the phone constantly and had my lists at the ready almost like an extra appendage. At one point during the onset of our business, Frank's boss lived on our block. Certainly, there was no law against launching an Amway business, but we really didn't want to give the impression that Frank was anything but entirely devoted to his job—a company man, you know. I used to do my darndest to make sure the UPS truck was not outside the house for too long. So, on top of everything else I was doing, I tried to be discreet about the business and the way it was taking off. It's funny looking back, we were a living sitcom.

There were none of these bluish-gray smiley vans like today. If you were an independent Amway business owner your days were dictated by the UPS pickup and delivery schedule—like clockwork. I mean if you missed him—well, you just didn't dare miss him—that was your reputation on the line. Your customers were depending on you, waiting for you to come through with their favorite vitamins, lotions, cleaning products, and what have you.

I have no earthly idea what the inside of an Amazon factory looks like. But let me tell you, inside the Underwood house, shelves were stacked, products were grouped, and orders were moving and grooving. And we had our shipping station with tape, boxes, and the packing popcorn. If someone trusted us enough to place orders, you better believe the Underwoods were not going to disappoint.

Once the kids were squared away each morning, I started buzzing about. It was exciting and rewarding. The way Frank and I saw it, we were building a legacy, not just a business. And thankfully, it worked. That's what it all became.

Now certainly, I know that people have a lot of opinions about Amway. Many simply don't understand it, if you ask me. A company that grows into the number one direct selling company in the world must be doing something right! It's not like it's some fly-by-night organization. It was founded in 1959, for goodness' sake. Just to give some context to the growth I talk about, you have to realize—Frank and I weren't the only people to experience Amway success. We're not a fluke. The organization really hit a chord with millions of people just like us. In 1980, the company had global sales of about

$1 billion, which was a half million more than just two years prior. By 1988, sales reached nearly $2 billion. And by 2013, Amway's worldwide sales were $11.8 billion.

You didn't misread—I'm talking billions with a *B*. The success is documented for anyone to see. Still there are people who dismiss the power of the business, those who look down on the structure of multilevel marketing.

I think I know where some of the skepticism comes from though. Amway, at its core, is built on relationships. It's remarkable to me only because the principles of Amway success are so very simple: We really are our brothers' keeper after all. See, to get this business model you have to be able to conceive of a strong community; and you have to be able to conceive of success through community, which is difficult for some folks, I suppose. In the common "me, me, me" value system we have throughout our culture today, the notion of community has been lost. And sadly, a whole lot of people operate in a kind of victim mentality—a defeatist attitude that warps their perception and blocks their blessings. They're trapped, stuck in a jail almost, of their own making.

Listen when I tell you—that old saying is true: "You can only achieve what your mind can conceive and your heart can believe." Frank and I live those words and raised our children by them. They are rooted in our family values. We wholeheartedly believe in the power of big thinking and hard work.

To my mind, Amway work is different from work-work. In some ways, I'm not even sure that *work* is the best word to define it. Yes, it takes up a lot of my time. And, yes, it was tiring and seemingly endless at times.

If there was one word to best sum up what Frank and I were doing, it would have to be: *building*.

And when you think about it, even at its most basic level, building is planning and leading. When you were a kid playing with a LEGO set, you had to make sure the bottom—your foundation—was secure, right? And each new piece had to align with the pieces underneath. If not, your structure would very quickly topple. It's not rocket science, but it is skillful and it does require intention.

But even a child's mind has an awe-filled eye on the finished product. So there is a joy and sense of fulfillment that comes from erecting that tower or that airplane—whatever it is you yourself have envisioned comes with great satisfaction as you bring it closer and closer to fruition. So much so that you don't fret or agonize over the steps it takes to get you there.

Everything is in the eye of the beholder. Some people might say, "Oh gosh, Amway means you have to constantly go out and sell all the time and always look to recruit new people." That's one way of looking at it. In my view, I'm out here offering people a way to take greater charge of their lives—start their own business and develop an added income stream by selling amazing, exclusive products that people actually need anyway.

We aren't out here trying to get people to buy spaceships or some kind of newfangled items or gimmicks. These are high-quality, life-enhancing items that most families use every day: nutrition supplements, lotion, and deodorant. And what I really love is that the products are made naturally with botanicals and other simple ingredients. You can feel good about bringing these products into your home, using them on your children. All any of us want is to take care of our family the best we can. Right? Amway helps do just that.

When I meet and talk to people, if they express interest in learning more about Amway—and I'm talking about people who have an understanding of their goals in life, in other words, their "why"—we arrange a meeting where we show The Plan, a standard step company wide. Basically, it means that the Amway business model is formally explained and laid out.

Every leader has their own personal spin on the presentation. Of course, I'm partial to Frank's style; it weaves in his faith, family, and patriotism. Like many people he shares some of the experiences that have shaped his life. I think his military background and what has motivated him as he served the country and moved up the ranks of army leadership truly captivate an audience. You can literally see how he touches people's lives and inspires them. His success helps illustrate how far a commitment to God and family and country can take you.

Beyond the personal flavor, the important takeaways of The Plan include a willingness to be coached and mentored, as well as having discipline and shared values of financial stewardship and independence. People will often say to themselves, "Oh I want to be my own boss." And that's a good thing. Clearly, business ownership is key to working for yourself, making your money, and building your future. But the key to making time *and* money is duplication, scaling that business. This sets Amway apart. You see, you're leveraging your efforts through teams.

The people in our organization are hands down the reason we found success.

Even now, at the point where I can't get around like I want, I spend my days on the phone, checking in on my friends and their children. And I go through stationery like nobody's business. I love sending and receiving notes. Sometimes just to say, "Hello, I'm thinking of you."

We were in steady communication with our partners—so much so that in the thick of it, we all knew how to support one another. When they say "teamwork makes the dream work," there are no truer words. You need that solid foundation of trust and love, if you ask me, to make the business grow. There was nothing formally written that said wives do this in Amway and husbands do that. But many of us wives, even if employed outside the home, had some degree of flexibility in our day.

Frank and I, quite naturally, developed a division of labor that made the best sense for us and our family. Everyone's breakdown will look different. Some folks are dual-worker households, and the work of one partner complements the work of the other.

A lot of the time, during my day I'm talking to wives much like myself. And since we all enjoy a close friendship, the business part felt seamless. Here's how it basically broke down on most days:

Mondays: Orders were called in. Remember absolutely everything was done by hand. So I kept a running list of all the things customers wanted and needed. The folks in our organization would let me know the orders to fulfill. We had a *lot* of downline sellers. So the order process could easily take up most of the day.

Tuesdays: We'd "show The Plan" each week. Often it was Frank. Depending on the number of people I recruited, that might mean a few couples coming over to the house. As our business grew, though, it usually meant renting a hotel conference room. Now, any Amway person worth their salt is always selling. Not products necessarily, although that's important. You learn quickly that your success is built on empowering the success of others. So whether you're at the supermarket, a PTA meeting, a church social, or what have you, you are always attuned to sharing your Amway story with people who might be like-minded. If your chat yielded some interest on their part, you'd invite them to learn more in a bit more formal setting to see The Plan. I had to plan for showing The Plan: reserve a space, arrange refreshments, and such.

Wednesdays: This was ground zero for logistics and fulfillment, although we didn't call it that. You have to remember there was no online component, no computers. So on Wednesdays the products ordered were delivered to our house. The products got divided up, then came the elbow grease. You see, the items had to be shipped upline to all the legs within our organization. Those who lived locally would come by the house to pick up the items their customers wanted. And they'd gather up the products, put them in the trunk of their car, and all day people were coming and going like that.

I needed to think ahead to avoid utter chaos—
although sometimes it may have looked like
havoc. I had a list of what went to whom, as did
each of the sales people.

Thursdays: Items needed to be ready for
shipping directly to customers. This is when all
the Styrofoam peanuts got poured and boxes
were taped and taped and taped some more!

Fridays: I took great pleasure in all the days we
spent building the business. But I really enjoyed
the time spent preparing for end-of-the-week
meetings. They were in-person, of course.
And Frank and I really looked at it as a time of
fellowship. We made it a point to come up with
ways to connect with our people, of course—
but also to engage their minds and enrich their
spirits. There might be guest speakers or maybe
we'd discuss a book, or a Bible passage. After
all, nothing can grow without being fed. This
was a really special time.

I am so grateful that Frank and I discovered Amway, and not just for the financial benefits. It gave us a vehicle to put into practice what God had purposed for our lives. I sincerely believe that be it in business or church or family, Frank and I were placed on earth for service leadership. From that first meeting years ago in Buffalo, our faith has held us together in so many ways. When people say they've grown under our leadership, that's a high compliment. And one I don't take lightly. We are equally yoked, Frank and I. We have a mutual understanding of our responsibilities as Christ followers.

None so profound as leading through service. I know I probably sound like an old fogy and a broken record. But I am really saddened by the lost biblical principles my generation was raised on. Certainly, I admire success. And individuals' riches have grown mightily in modern times. But you have to ask: What is it based on? What does it mean? How does it add to His kingdom?

Like anyone, I am flattered when people pay me compliments: "Oh, Marilyn, you're a wonderful leader." They may admire the way I wear my makeup or style my hair. I'm glad if other women admire my fashion sense or the way I carry myself. I just hope they realize it's all God, from which all blessings flow.

It is clear to me that by blessing us with a position where we have influence, God intends for me to use all my gifts to help others. It's no accident that Amway has been part of our life's journey. The life of a servant leader is all about growth. There are many, many elements to servant leadership. And they really all mirror the life of Jesus Christ on earth; the examples are in the Bible. I am only doing what the Word has taught: serving with integrity and love.

When it comes to our business, I know—and Frank agrees—this status only comes from living biblically. We are so proud of our Amway Emerald ranking. It signifies more than a dollar or point value—although that is important. Lots of independent business owners meet sales targets. Emeralds have established a growing and sustainable organization *and* built a culture of support within your team. In other words, we are very successful and so are lots of the people we mentor. So we are qualified Platinum leaders and downline, the legs we have sponsored have each hit performance bonus levels as well.

The average Emerald earns more than $125,000 annually in gross revenue—that's according to Amway data, not just me talking. The exact amount will vary, depending on the size of the team, the volume the team does—and, of course, the consistency. What matters most to Frank and me is that Emerald status is impossible to reach unless the independent business owners on your team achieve financial success as well.

And it's nothing that can happen overnight. Amway status is determined by a steady record of volume, not a good hit or sales bump here and there. It takes years of time, effort, and dedication to learning and investing in people's personal and spiritual fulfillment.

Although Amway is still a big part of our lives, it's

obviously not like the past—when we were younger. I miss those days. I miss being outside. So much to do. So many places to go—things I had to do. Was it hectic? Sure. Was I doing too much? You bet. But I loved it.

There were days I'd be planning coursework for Mellisa, my youngest. See, I homeschooled Baby Girl. I'd be running to the grocery store to get dinner together. Blair loved my spaghetti. The whole family did. But he was especially thrilled to come home from school and smell that sauce on the stove. And I wanted the house to be just so by the time Frank came home from work.

Not only because I wanted to honor my role as a wife and mother. Honestly, Frank and I needed our evenings free. Sometimes we had Bible study. Frank continued to teach Sunday school throughout our marriage, and I served as choir director. And with the business, there was always something going on; if there wasn't an event set on the calendar, we were more than likely planning for one.

We made sure, in our organization, that there were frequent times of fellowship. One event I took great pride in was Underwood Family Day. It was a wonderful annual time—usually in early fall—of games and swimming and, of course, good food. We often hosted Family Day at Hershey Park or maybe in the tranquil Pocono Mountains; the venue would change up. Most important, we got a site with something to offer for kids of all ages. You see, we knew and understood that our independent business owners worked hard.

And think about it—why were they devoting so much time and energy to Amway? For most of us, our "why" is centered on our children. It was very important to Frank and me that the little ones had a sense of what their parents were part of—the excitement and joy of it. This way, business ownership on some level would perhaps become something they could see themselves doing. We all want a better life for our children and their children. It's human nature. But how many of us are being intentional about showing our children what that looks like?

Of course, that's the underlying motive. But each element of the day was focused on kids and playtime. On Family Day, we deliberately scheduled no sales or training sessions. It was all about fun—a chance for all of our children to meet one another, and for parents to relax, knowing their kids were safe, entertained, fed, and celebrated. There were lots of elements that went into it, lots of coordinating the moving pieces so that it came off well. We'd hire clowns and other performers. The children loved different food stations, too—cotton candy was a huge hit.

Then, roughly three times a year Frank and I hosted an adult trip for our organization—maybe a conference, a training, or just a fun escape for twenty or thirty couples. Acapulco was a really popular destination, everyone loved it, and we went there often. Our biggest pleasure came from taking care of the independent business owners in our line. In corporate America, I think companies often say their people are their strongest asset. And I'm sure they mean it. Frank and I wanted to do more than say "you're important"—we wanted to show folks how much they're valued.

I laugh sometimes thinking that in another life, I was maybe an event or party planner. These events were a real highlight for me. Nothing set my heart on fire quite like Christmastime. I hosted several affairs throughout the holidays—at least three Christmas parties for our Amway family. And when I tell you I go all out, you better believe I mean it.

I get such joy out of decorating: Christmas trees were everywhere, as many as a hundred large and small; holly along the mantel, and even around the guest bathroom vanity. And I really enjoyed assembling gifts for everyone. One year, I found the most beautiful Christmas plates you've ever seen, at a dollar store of all places! I kept a lookout for special items fifty-two weeks a year. And back in the good old days, before every store was part of a huge chain, you could find special, beautiful things where you'd least expect it. I had a drawer filled with cloth napkins I'd collected and I'd discovered lovely and unusual centerpieces. Always, I had these events catered—not because I didn't love to cook. I did. But I wanted to make sure our folks felt special. To me, that meant giving them my full attention and a sit-down meal with someone serving their needs.

It is so gratifying to hear people talk about the fun they had. Or sometimes one of the ladies might say: "Marilyn, where'd you get that serving dish?" or "What was that appetizer?"

That meant a lot. It was as though people somehow could carry the beauty of our shared time together with them.

Now the good Lord knows, I cannot say I saw this life for myself. But, on some level, I suppose I had a sense—even as a girl coming up in Buffalo—that I would do something enterprising. I would run something. Maybe that's why as a teen I walked around my little all-girls high school dressed like a career woman—or what that looked like to fifteen-year-old Marilyn. There wasn't a clear-cut vision of the future. But I was going to be dressed for it!

The simple sheath dress was what I could afford to put together from a simple McCalls pattern and a couple of yards of fabric. It was also intrinsically sophisticated in its simplicity. My kitten heel shoes said sophisticated but also read practical. And, of course, we can't forget my clipboard and briefcase. Looking back, I couldn't tell you what I carried in it. Maybe my notebooks? It wasn't for show, I'll tell you that. I think I was just always serious about myself.

And even then I wanted the world to know that Marilyn was in charge, ready to get the job done. I mention all this to say that I didn't just *want* more from life, I saw it. Every day when I left the little bungalow Mother rented for us, I now know that I was stepping out on faith. The very definition—the substance of things hoped for; evidence of things not seen—is clearly what drove me. I had surely not witnessed a Black woman holding a seat in business. That's for sure. I suppose I thought, "Well, why not me?" I have to hand it to Mother, though. She never questioned or dampened my ambitions—whether she understood them or not. From where she came from, and the life she'd led—where your race and your gender put you in a box—it would've been perfectly understandable for her to say: "Now, Marilyn. That's not what ladies are expected to do." Or, "Whites won't allow a Black person to do such and such."

Nope. She just watched me and listened to my hopes and dreams. If she ever doubted me, she didn't let it show. Never said, "Girl, where do you think you're going dressed like that? Why don't you go off to school like the other teens in the neighborhood?" My small circle of friends and I just knew we had it going on.

In a small way, even then I wanted to influence people in a positive way—to stand out. Not in a prideful way, really more as a means of self-expression. For as long as I can remember, I've wanted more. To me, excellence is a way to honor God. How do we as Christ followers take what He has given us—and steward that in a way that builds something up?

The truth of the matter is, I don't really have an answer. In the doing, you don't ask yourself a lot of questions. You simply do what needs to be done.

I have loved being Frank Underwood's wife. I was blessed to have my four children. And, while I certainly enjoyed Amway, it was all the more special because of the partnership I had with my husband.

It was ours.

We built it.

We nurtured it.

We grew it—together.

Now, what I will say, without hesitation, is that we were able to succeed because of our strong Christian faith. There is an amazing book that illustrates so eloquently our shared belief in *The Power of the Blood*. Now, I suppose that's not news to most believers. We all know that the blood of Jesus Christ holds untold power. But a lot of us forget that we can tap into that power in our everyday lives. It's written by H. A. Maxwell Whyte, and I've gifted it to more people in our organization than I can count. To a person, they are changed by it.

The lessons and the way the author presents them are, I believe, especially noteworthy when it comes to life and family, even business. Frank and I have borne witness to the results—well, more than mere results, miracles really—that take place in your life once you know how to tap into that secret weapon: the power in His blood. Spiritually, it's a gamechanger, let me tell you, to realize how it can energize and empower you. And, goodness, I'm not the only one moved by these principles. I think that book has sold over a half million copies! At its core, it's about a profound understanding of spiritual warfare. There's an old hymn by the same name, and I remember it from my own childhood back in Buffalo. But coming up back then, we sang about the Holy Spirit and the blood as a way to highlight what we as Christians could look *forward* to. No one I knew talked about it as something to be experienced on earth, in the here and now. This is what folks miss.

My husband has a wonderful way of expanding on it. And oh, people really are so moved by the way he breaks it down. A lot of the power in Frank's expressions have to do with the strength of his charismatic delivery. You see, Frank has a way! When he walks into a room, there's the sway of his officer training that commands it, but he somehow envelops that in a very engaging warmth at the same time. He is truly a man of steel and velvet. Everybody says so, not just me. And it's true.

What my husband is saying—the words coming out of his mouth—mixed with a particular cadence and resonance. We both know that a lot of nonbelievers think he is simply a very good orator, a kind of motivational speaker—spouting off on the benefits of positive thinking. But it's so much more than that. In our business model, the way it all unfolds, is we play off one another. Not in a contrived way; it's perfectly natural. We just have a rhythm, I suppose you might call it.

We are truly a perfect team. Often in a marriage, you'll find the wife following her husband's lead. And I think there is great honor in that, respecting your covenant. It's a blessing that I don't have to consciously remind myself to follow Frank. We both want the same things, and we see life and our faith in much the same way.

We both wear a lot of hats in the business. But most often, I am serving as the recruiter, if you will. I introduce people to the concept of the business. Now, this is very simple for me—not even work, really. Because I really do believe in the goodness, value, and utmost high quality of Amway products and the family-based principles of the organization. So I talk to people, as I would normally, about this and that. I'm naturally curious. So as I'm talking with people at the grocery store or maybe on the sidelines of the boys' football games, they might mention something they're dealing with in their lives. And in my heart of hearts I believe Amway can help them.

Am I leading people to the business? Yes, of course. But the way I see it, I am more so connecting with folks.

Pearl of Leadership

Success in business is like success in life: thousands of small, sometimes seemingly insignificant steps. The center of business growth is people. Plain and simple. If you don't have great people alongside you, folks you can nurture and coach—who have the same vision you have and value the connection you share—then who are you actually leading? You have to be able to conceive of success through community.

Mom and Dad at the Gold Rush Days party, 1974, Fort Carson, Colorado.

8

FAITH

One day I started to notice it really clearly. I had been aware on some level. But I really stopped one day and said to myself, "Now *this* is different." Being saved is one thing but now He is doing a brand-new thing. That's the only way I can explain it. I love my Bible—always loved scripture. But life took a turn and I could see it, feel it, know it. "I'm not just reading the word. I am *in* the word." Does that make sense? I'm talking about experiencing the presence of God in a totally new light.

This was in the 1980s, and the renewal I experienced was not coming from a backslider position, although—praise God—there is no shame in falling short as a

Christian of the glory of God. This is real life we are living and He is a merciful king. Scripture teaches us that there is no condemnation for those who are in Jesus Christ. We simply cannot be separated from His love.

No, I was functioning in my faith the way I always had: praying and praising. The way the reawakening all came about, let me tell you, was quite a journey. I'm talking about a really scary time. Because, again, it's not like I didn't know the Bible. But—and I know I'm not the first to experience this—sometimes God will take you through something. He has to. We won't like it. Won't understand it. But it's all part of His purpose. To get you to a new level.

Let me back up a little. See, Frank and I had been in the business for like, two or three months. Our Amway sales were going very well. Yes, it was hectic, but I was truly loving the new chapter of our lives. We were partnering in a whole new way in our marriage. I found it so exciting, because the children were getting bigger and more self-sufficient, and our entire family was beginning to shift into a new direction. Moms will know what I'm talking about. One day you wake up and realize, "Oh, I have a house full of big kids—preadolescents and teens. There is no more doing every little thing. They each have chores, responsibilities, and they are starting to come into their own.

When Amway came into our lives, it was perfect because I could have a new place to put that energy. I could nurture a new baby—a business. And that was a desire inside me that had been long dormant. One thing about me: I'm going to leap at the chance to build something. That gets me jazzed up. Amway was growing.

Then, out of the blue, I started losing sight in my left eye. No apparent reason. And it happened in a flash, really. I experienced something similar sometime in the late 1970s. I hadn't really talked about what happened to my sight years ago—headaches, then the peripheral vision fading. This was different. There was no leading up to it. I didn't have any headaches to speak of. It felt as though someone, somehow, was playing with the light switch in my head: darkness, then a faint glimmer, and darkness again.

Doctors I went to, and it felt like one appointment after another, were scratching their heads, because they couldn't figure it out. Then I went to Bethesda Naval Hospital—and even then it wasn't till after about fifteen trips. Finally they landed on what they called optic neuritis.

I'd never heard tell, of course. But I suppose if you can get arthritis in your body—well, then maybe in the eye the same kind of muscle thing is possible. I can't say I understood it. The doctors, even once they were able to give me a diagnosis, were not super clear in their own understanding. The human body is a mystery. That's for sure. I had felt a kind of tightness along the side of my face and the pressure was in my eye. That's the shorthand version of how it was explained to me. Any kind of way they tried to describe it, whether the cause—which they were not sure of—or the remedy—no answers really. I have to tell you, I can be a bit calmer about it all now. But the whole episode was very distressing. I mean, extremely so.

It really set me back on my heels and made me begin to think: "Hey, you know, Marilyn. You might lose sight in the other eye. And then what?"

I can't remember if I voiced my feelings to Frank or anyone in the family. But it really scared me. And having that fear—the thought of deep worry—scared me even further. Because it was very difficult to get past the idea of being blind. "How would I live my life?" I thought. Well, that's just the thing—it would mean I could not live my life, at least not as I'd known my life to be.

What spooked me more? I was taught that worry was the opposite of faith. And no matter how I tried to justify it in my mind, here I was: consumed with worry. So for the very first time in my entire life I was facing something that was causing me to question my belief.

I thought I was a Christian. I really did. So what did this mean?

If I were as strong in the Lord as I always thought I

was, it wouldn't have upset me. Right? So I sat with all of this warring inside me. To my mind, I had been faithful. No one is perfect, of course. But I really did believe myself to be walking in Christ. And at some point after questioning myself over and over again, I decided that maybe the Lord had just suddenly said: *Hmmm, let's wake Marilyn up. She's comfortable with life, and things seem to be going smoothly. It's time for a test.*

Sometimes, He has to sort of shock you a little bit. I believe that. Get your full attention. During that period I began to double down and get down to business. I was able to keep everyone's Amway orders moving along—almost like a robot, really. But the interest wasn't there. I hid it on the outside, but inside I started feeling sorry for myself. I was thinking about me, my life as a wife and as a mom, losing sight in both my eyes.

After a couple weeks of being—well, there's no other word for it—*stuck* in self-pity, I began to come around a bit. And what I decided on was almost a mission—to really, really read the Bible. I mean to the point of nearly eating and drinking the words. At the same time, I just kept on praying for the Lord to forgive me. Because even as I was reading so hard, it felt like maybe the sight was going in the other eye. I was deeply afraid at this point, but I didn't let up. I tell you the truth, I was reading like that funny cartoon character—you know the ostrich-looking thing? The Road Runner!

I was zooming from verse to verse, chapter to chapter. And it was sinking in a little bit more. Truly, I was discovering new elements that—maybe I hadn't exactly missed but took on more powerful significance.

Even with my sight slowly failing, Frank and I decided to move—only about two miles from where we were, but still. So my eyesight worries had to be put to the back burner while we coped with this move. So naturally there was a lot going on. Because any move is a big deal. Whether it's two miles or two hundred miles, the steps to prepare don't really change. And, don't forget, we are still introducing our new business. No one knew about all that was going on behind the scenes—you know, like my sight and the doctors and you know, the angst, so much angst.

There was a neighbor across the street who came over and introduced herself, and she was very nice—lovely really—and she was a Christian. But she came on a little bit too strong, I thought. Because I consider myself a strong Christian, so it was a bit off-putting at first to be on the receiving end of such aggressive evangelism. And in the beginning I may have missed what she was trying to get at. I'm not proud of it, but I truly almost missed out on something monumental because I wasn't ready for that kind of delivery. I can admit that now. She was persistent—and just kept inviting, and inviting, and inviting me to her church, and I'd said,

"No, we have a church." We did, of course, and I was happy with our church. I taught Sunday school, and I directed the junior choir and so forth—it was my happy place. Now, I guess she'd invited us about five times. And one week she was going to a Bible study class and she casually said, "Why don't you come along?" I don't know why, but the idea of studying the Bible was just a better entry point for me. When she was suggesting I come to Sunday service, it was a bridge too far. And maybe on some level, that carried a hint of betrayal to my home church. Frank and I had responsibilities at our church, and I couldn't be a no-show and just let down the people we regularly ministered—in the choir or the deacon board. Studying felt safe. Who among us can't benefit from studying? And I really have always enjoyed taking a text and looking at it in all kinds of different ways.

So I agreed to come along with her. And it was at *that* group study where I met her minister.

He was just teaching and breaking down this one passage—one that I had read close to a thousand times—in a way that shook me to my core. Okay, so we all know that in the Gospel of John, Jesus performed a very public and dramatic miracle when He blessed five loaves and two fishes, right? This is one of the miracles most Christians learn about pretty early on in their walk, and it is, of course, very important. He said "bring them hither to me" while the multitudes sat themselves down on the grass. They were hungry, and there was clearly not enough to feed them. Jesus did not send them home for supper now, did he? And remember the boy is pretty frantic because there is simply not enough food for five thousand people. The way I was always taught—obviously there's a lot of subtext and, like any of the parables, you can really go in on the symbolism. But the main point here is to help us understand how we need to trust in the Lord.

And that's what I took away for years. God will provide. That is very rich, and it is clear to any believer. And we can't forget that He didn't simply make sure there was just enough food—that would've been an amazing feat, of course. But ample provision is a fraction of what our God will do. Can I get an "Amen"? Don't forget there were twelve baskets left over.

Like anything, there's more than one way to consider the passage. Here's what happened that night: We read the passage John 6:8–13. And that young pastor proceeded to illustrate, not just that we need to trust God to provide, but also that He will take our little bit—be it what you have in limited ability, talent, faith—and when you give that over to Him, it will be blessed and multiplied many times over. See, so often we talk ourselves out of a challenge. We tell ourselves we don't have what it takes because we didn't go to college or we don't have the pedigree. What I learned in that Wednesday Bible study—led with such an anointing—is that John is telling us: Just bring it to Him. Pray and approach God with your meager contribution, but undying faith, and He will use you to do abundantly and exceedingly more than you ever dreamed possible.

I listened and learned—then he preached, in a way I just knew I wanted to be ministered. And I knew it was what I wanted for our family, each of our children to be taught. That's how blown away I was.

It wasn't long before I rededicated my life to Christ. As much as I'd always dug in and soaked in scripture, this was different. I started to discover meaning beyond the meaning I once understood—peeling back layer upon layer of understanding and purpose. It's really amazing, almost like seeing the sun and the clouds for the first time—when you are living your life and thinking you're one way. And then you're jolted a little bit and you see things differently, discovering that maybe you aren't as strong as you thought you were. It can be disorienting, that's for sure. But we have to realize that is exactly where God wants us. There's that irony, right? Because the word tells us that it is in our weakness that we are made strong.

Of course, everyone who knew me had pretty much always known me as a saved person. But there was something about the second time when I accepted, and I don't know what it was. My life began to change—almost on a cellular level, if that makes sense. The things I thought about, said, and did. Everything about life felt lighter. There was a peace I cannot put into words. Frank saw it in me. And that's the best testament, really. That there must be something there if somebody, and not just anybody but the person closest to you, can sense the shift in you.

One day my husband actually looked at me and said, "Whatever it is, I want it, too." You know how heavy it is for your husband of twenty-plus years to tell you that? Mind you, I had stopped talking about it at this point. Not because I was any less enthusiastic. More because I was so entrenched in my own spiritual path. God was working in me and through me. And, maybe for the first time, I'd totally surrendered to it. I thought I'd always lived in that fashion, but this was as though I had unlocked a greater level of trust.

Usually when I get energized about something, Frank knows he's going to hear about it. I know my husband, and I know he's not one to church hop. When it comes to church he has always said, "Well, Marilyn, you don't flip around to different churches. You're supposed to settle on a church home and be rooted in that ministry."

I felt the same way. Truly I did. But at the same time, I couldn't deny what was happening in my spirit. I mean, I was working so hard—we both were. But somehow it didn't feel like hard work. Our business kept growing. And you know what? My sight had been gone for six months and it came back.

I guess I got so busy just thinking about other people, the clients, our network. Then you know I was driving one day—now, I hadn't been able to drive for a while—but I just got in the car one day and I said, "I can really see!" You know it just sort of crept up on me. Mind you, I could never—well, at least for the last I guess five or ten years before that happened—really drive at night. I could try to drive, but everything was blurry: the streetlights, the road. Well now I see better than I ever saw before. Much clearer than ever before. That's a blessing. You just can't imagine what a blessing it was. While the Lord had me busy touching other people, he brought my sight back—and the business grew and grew.

My experience convinced Frank to visit the church, and he did. Wouldn't you know it, he saw and felt the same thing I did. And so we did it. We joined. And I don't know, maybe a month or so went by and Frank accepted Christ—rededicated, just as I had done. And we joined the church in Alexandria. And what was so beautiful was that our children saw it. We didn't really talk about it. The children saw something happening in us and they—one by one—were moved. And each child, one by one, accepted Christ on their own.

It was what they did on their own; nobody prodded them. That was a really special time in our lives as parents. You know, I'll tell you: When you know the Lord and then you start a family you are keenly aware of the huge responsibility you have for these sweet little souls He created through you. It's very heavy. You can take your children to church. You can have them recite the Bible, chapter and verse. But, truly, they must form their own spiritual relationship with God—and there's not a darn thing you can do about it, as a mom or dad, if they don't want that for themselves.

As for me, I knew from my own mother and how she raised me, you have to pray every day that He would live in you and live through you. It's really the only way to make God real in the lives of those you touch.

Let's start back in Buffalo, where I was born. My mother had no education. She had no husband. It's something I don't talk about very often. But the fact is, my parents were not only not together, but my dad was never a part of my life. Ever. I believe I was the product of an affair between my parents. And shortly after I was born, my dad moved to Canada—you know it's a short distance from Buffalo. Certainly, for a Black man in the 1930s there was more opportunity and less harsh discrimination over there compared with the US—not the constant brutality of racism that Black Americans lived with. The point I am making though is he abandoned my mother and me.

He had a younger brother, Uncle Lee, who made it his business to be a sort of positive male figure in my life. It wasn't like a constant father-like love. But he'd check on Mother and me occasionally. And we had a familial relationship. I think he felt bad for my mom, and perhaps a bit ashamed of his brother's negligence. He always had an encouraging word and a ready smile.

Mom was welcoming when Uncle Lee came to visit. But I know my mother, and I'm sure she never asked him for a red cent. She would just keep on keeping on, working from job to job and taking care of us the best she could. And I feel bad about it now as an adult, but I can recall stressing her out. At maybe around eight or nine years old, I was whining: "Why can't I have four frilly dresses?" "Why must I have only one pair of dress up shoes?"

I had no idea how hard things were for her. She had something great on her side though. That I do know: Mother knew the Lord. 'Cause if it hadn't been for that, I don't think she would've gotten through, and I probably wouldn't have survived either. As far as I could see, there was not even an ounce of anger in her heart, even though her circumstances as a single mother were terribly harsh. No one would have blamed her for being angry, but I never heard a cross word out of her mouth about being abandoned and having to struggle as we did.

Uncle Lee was a good man. And I believe it meant something to my mother that at least one person in my dad's family acknowledged us. As an adult, Uncle Lee and I stayed in touch—writing and calling off and on. He had a relationship with the kids. And he'd visit us now and again. Not until after some years, Frank was stationed at Fort Carson and we were living in Colorado Springs, did my uncle say to me, out of the blue: "You know you have a sister?"

I thought, "Uncle Lee, what in the world are you talking about?" You have to understand, my mother had poured into me so much—as did our community in Buffalo—that I never longed for, or considered, that "family" might be more than the people I saw every day. Yes, I wanted to create a nuclear family for my own children. But as for me—little girl Marilyn—emotionally, God had long ago given me peace about that. I didn't want for love—had plenty.

Uncle Lee had stoked my curiosity. He asked if I wanted to meet my father, and I was all for the idea. Come to find out, my dad had a wife and, just like me, three children: two boys and a girl. Mellisa hadn't been born yet, though his children were full-grown. And my father was very open to the idea of meeting. Uncle Lee worked out the details, and before long we were reunited.

It was like a full-circle moment for me, because I felt an instant connection. And I could sense that my dad had a lot of respect for the way I'd turned out, with Frank, and our family. In the years that followed I traveled to spend time with my stepsiblings and their children. My dad came to see me and my children. It was a very beautiful turn of events—a blessing I could've never even dreamed up.

And the way Jesus kept me all those years—first with my mom and then with Frank—there was no room in my heart for bitterness or resentment. I'm grateful for that. My father may have left me, but God never abandoned me. His spirit is so full of grace and mercy that by walking with him, that was in my heart as well.

Now, let's not forget, we are human beings. And while we can recognize some of what the Holy Spirit is doing in the supernatural—believe you me, none of the Lord's grace stopped my husband from having a few choice words! I didn't hear the conversation. All I know is Frank, at one point, pulled my dad aside and told him: "Look here, I know you're her father. But I'm her husband. And if you hurt her, you'll have to deal with *me*."

That's my Frank—a soldier, a gentleman, a man of God. But don't mess with him. You hear me?

Pearl of Faith

We need to trust in the Lord. God will take you through something. He has to. We won't like it. Won't understand it. But it's all part of His Purpose. To get you to a new level. I started to notice it really clearly. I could see it, feel it, know it. "I'm not just reading the Word. I am in the Word." God will provide. Just bring it to Him. Pray and approach God with your meager contribution, but undying faith, and He will use you to do abundantly and exceedingly more than you ever dreamed possible.

Mom and Dad at his retirement ceremony in Fort Lee, Virginia, 1982.

9

DUTY

It's funny. But after nearly fifty years I find myself going back to a simple little paperback book that just about rocked my world from the time I picked it up. For those who don't know *Jonathan Livingston Seagull*, you're missing out. It's a thin, children's-looking book—barely a hundred pages. And it's illustrated, with remarkably simple—yet enthralling—black-and-white pictures. Each time I reread it, somehow the words are more and more meaningful.

There are times, when I lie here, unable to move much at all—with my body—that some of the lessons nearly move me to tears.

I'd never heard of the author until the book came out and began flying off the shelves. I don't think he was a celebrated writer. And I suppose that's the beauty of his particular way of telling a story. I always loved losing myself in a good book. But this one was so unlike anything I'd ever come across. First of all, whoever heard of a lowly seagull as a main character? Not an eagle, all majestic and fascinating. Or even a cardinal or a bluebird—beautiful birds, right? The kind of elegant creatures everyone loves. Let's face it, most people find seagulls to be sort of disgusting. They're not beautiful. They don't sing. What is that loud annoying sound they make anyway? They just scavenge for food—and any scrap of food just about, like vultures.

But from the very first page, I was hooked into this odd bird—Jonathan Livingston Seagull. What the thing looked like on the page was nothing like the gross things swooping down to bother you on a beach. Straightaway, as I read the words, Jonathan Livingston Seagull was me—working itself into a state. He was concentrating and concentrating on something we all know comes naturally to birds: flying. While all the other seagulls are focused on grabbing a leftover burger or something from the garbage, he's fretting over the intricacies of stretching and twisting his wings just so. The goal is the curve that will give him perfect gliding.

And no one in his seagull world gets it. The other

seagulls clearly see him as this oddity. Some kind of weirdo. And his poor parents worry that if he doesn't let go of this wild obsession of his, consumed by something as unimportant as flying, then he won't have enough food to make it through the winter.

The dad says to him what the mom is probably also thinking, something like: "Look, flying is not the point; we only fly so we can eat." So out of respect for his parents, Jonathan Livingston Seagull was obedient—or at least as obedient as he could be—and he started diving for bread crusts and other food scraps. But he never gave up his pursuit to live his seagull life as beautifully and joyfully as possible. To me, it was as though he'd made up his mind—"Okay, if we have to fly, I'm going to make it mean something—I won't just fly, I'll soar."

Seems silly to admit how much I—a Black girl from Buffalo, New York—took to it. Immediately. And I still relate to that odd-bird seagull named Jonathan Livingston. I don't care what anybody says, if we are honest, I think a part of all of us lives inside that bird. Flying can be a symbol for just about anything you need it to be. For some folks that means working your job as best you can. The way I interpret Jonathan's plight is a way of figuring out how to live this thing called life. Not through drudgery and robotic tasks, but with joy. Everyone knows that birds fly. But Jonathan wants to discover how to perfect his flying and squeeze every last bit of meaning and virtue out of his everyday existence. In other words—at least the way I see it—grab the extraordinary out of the ordinary.

Now, *Jonathan Livingston Seagull* is not meant to be religious instruction—at least I don't think it is. But if you have a soul, there is almost no way the story will not stir something inside. For me, Jonathan captures my life as a woman of God. After all, in a way he is also living his life as a way to reach "heaven"—but for him that's not a time or a place so much as it is a state of mind. Shouldn't we all be reaching our heaven? I know I am. Jesus is my Lord and Savior, and by living a life in obedience to God my eternal life is assured.

What does that look like here on earth though? Not many of us think about that. It's something I've considered for many years. Because if I am to be a doer of the word and not just a hearer of the word—like the scripture says in James's first chapter—that's a tall order, right? And I never wanted to be one of those legalistic Christians, almost performing His teachings. That's not enough. I have a duty to honor God. Excellence is the way to live up to His promise.

The last thing I intend to do is spoil the book for anyone who hasn't read it. But I guess the best way to sum up *Jonathan* and what the amazing fable shows us is: The path is already written—we just have to love and make a decision every single day to live in our truth. That's it. Pretty simple, when you break it down.

As a very little girl, I prayed God would one day give me a family to love and to cherish. And He answered my prayer.

It is my delight—and I mean, my *pure* delight—to worship Him. In my heart of hearts that's what the weird seagull is about for me; that's where it resonates. In the living of *my* life. The life God has given me. I worship and get meaning from serving my family—loving my family, being obedient to the will of God as a wife and mother.

Duty, like most words, means something different to everyone. My duty is my worship. It is my praise. Duty is obedience to God, and in my opinion, it's widely misunderstood—even by church folks, who feel strongly attached to their Christian faith. It isn't work in the way people often define *work*. This is something that is very, very hard to articulate. And most of the world cannot grasp it. I say that with love, not to diminish anyone's intelligence. If you have a spirit of unbelief, what I am saying, and the way I am living, will naturally make no sense whatsoever. For some reason, it's easier to look at me and say, "Oh, you know how Marilyn is—work, work, work—selfless and hopelessly devoted to her family."

But, in fact, there is nothing hopeless about my

devotion at all. My hope is in the Lord. And my "duty" is my blessing. It's in Psalm 33. It's written: "We put our hope in the Lord. He is our help and our shield. In Him our hearts rejoice..."

My own family and countless friends say all the time: "Rest, Marilyn—you're doing too much." I know they mean well, but I take to heart that saying "to whom much is given..." and this is who I am. My duty is not a burden. I realize that sacrifice is very foreign to some people, especially today. If they grew up the way I did, I think they might have a better understanding.

I admit I never understood the true meaning of sacrifice until I took a look back. It was many years before I finally realized what my mother had gone through—the burdens she shouldered. In silence. And it's fair to say that she modeled something that cannot be taught or lectured.

Think about it: Where would a woman, a Black woman at that, get the will to raise up a child into a world she could only see in her dreams? Imagine what she went through. And don't forget, I was born during the Depression, as if life for African Americans wasn't already tight enough. The Depression years were very challenging. Soup kitchens. Wide-scale poverty. My mom went from job to job—not because she was a bad worker. That was the nature of the economy we lived in. Of course, I was a child. I never had any frame of reference. And we're talking about a time when American culture was very different from what it is now—with all of our luxuries and conveniences. Well, I call them luxuries and conveniences: cell phones, microwave ovens, fancy TVs, websites, and all this. It's all basic today. No one thinks of them as extravagant.

I'm sometimes asked about the difficulties of being the wife of a serviceman. The moving all the time. The obligations. Yes, it's a fact: I married a soldier in the US Army. But when I think about it, I was raised by one of the finest soldiers this country has ever seen. My mother. I don't talk about it often, even to those closest to me. But think about how strong a Black woman of her time had to be to raise up a child with hope. I'm not talking about physically strong, although she was. I'm speaking about a strong spirit, someone so strong in the Lord that she would set out to do what no one had taught her to do: have and teach a child to dream when, all around you, the world never saw fit to honor your own dreams. And do it alone.

As a kid, I spent summers with my mother's parents, my grandparents in Lynchburg, Virginia. Words cannot express what a big deal it was. Because I know now some of what she went through. Now I understand it and how she raised me. If it hadn't been for the Lord on her side—well, I can't even begin to imagine. I don't think she would've gotten through and I probably wouldn't have either. I looked forward to my summer adventure. The out-of-the-world excitement for me was to get on the train. It may as well have been the Concord for all that it represented to me—freedom, luxury, grown-up stuff. I can remember from age seven on up to fifteen or so I traveled by myself. And I still remember that eerie feeling that came over me once I hit Washington, DC, entering the South and everything that meant.

And, baby, let me tell you that the climate changed from Buffalo to Lynchburg, and I'm not just talking about the temperature. I knew, with no one uttering a word of warning, that for the summer this little chocolate girl was going to live a very different lifestyle for the next three months. Not to say there was no prejudice in Buffalo or New York City—it was there, just different. But Lynchburg was a way of living where my skin color was pronounced and dictated what we did and where we went. Our "bathroom" was outside, okay? And I just rolled with it. I can't say I enjoyed every aspect, but for me, that was all part of the adventure.

I learned how to cook on a coal stove, believe it or not. I learned how to iron with the flat irons and learned how to iron handkerchiefs with a flat iron. I mean you haven't experienced anything unless you've learned how to iron with a flat iron.

And I used to go to the spring to get water. That's the best water you ever had—out of the ground, believe me.

And for two years, Mother let me stay in Lynchburg for my health because I used to have a terrible case, yearly, of bronchial asthma. And she thought for a year, maybe I could get out of that climate in Buffalo and live in Lynchburg and it would help me. So I went down and actually went to school there. Talk about an experience; imagine going to school in a two-room—you couldn't really call it a building—wooden structure.

So when I say I describe my mom, our little home in Buffalo—when I talk about my humble background, just know—that *humble*, in fact, is putting it mildly. I owe so much to the strong family I come from, who made great sacrifices for me. It's not something very many people can really wrap their brains around.

They see Marilyn Underwood, wife of an esteemed serviceman, mother of four amazing children, and so on. And I love my life as a wife and mother, for sure. Those of us who grew up in the church are probably familiar with a line—I think of it often, in fact the line's been put to song: "You don't know my story." And the message there is that on the outside folks can see the glory, but they don't know anything about the difficulties—all those messy, unglamorous parts—that got us to the glorious image.

I don't care what I'm wearing or where I'm going—a soup kitchen or the Isle of Capri—it's what's inside me that shapes me. The girl from Buffalo, the outhouse or two-room schoolhouse in Lynchburg, Virginia. That is who I am.

And, to be quite honest, I am still the Marilyn Scales who aspires to do and be more. Even at my age. And even with this dreadful disease. Something I probably haven't shared with very many people is that despite the wonderful years I spent in New York City at Traphagen School of Fashion and the beautiful life I've shared with Frank, I always wanted to be a college graduate. I love learning, love knowledge—always have. And I always saw myself in a classroom soaking up the teachings of a professor, studying, and writing papers. Don't ask me when or how I thought I'd fit college into my life, but I dreamed of a collegiate life.

And a small part of me has struggled, confidence-wise, for that lack of formal education. I realize that may seem silly. I know in my heart that it's not that I'm not intelligent. We all know some educated fools in the world. And a degree is not, in and of itself, a measure of knowledge. College has never been about proving anything or getting the academic world's validation. The mark of real intelligence, I believe, is curiosity. It's wonder, and a desire to be a student of life and letters. I can certainly hold my own in most discussions about world events or different philosophies. I just always wanted more—more scholarship, if you will.

If you don't know by now, once I get hold of some

kind of idea—no matter what it is—it's very hard for me to let it go. That's just who I am. I'm not a quitter. Never have been. So I don't think people close to me were all that surprised when I enrolled in an online college—at eighty-two years old!

I was a bit nervous—with excitement, more than fear. This was a step I had only dreamed of. To be honest, I never even imagined that there was such a thing as "online" college. I am still finding my way through all of the technology in the world nowadays. To think that a little thing the size of a wallet could be a phone. And not just a phone, but a phone book, encyclopedia, you name it. Now, I can certainly see that some people are way too attached to the cell phone. But I do like that I can use these gadgets now to reach out to my children and my grandchildren anytime I want.

Goodness, I never thought it would be possible to go to college without leaving my house. Blair was inspired when he'd given the commencement speech for a large online college, and he just knew I'd be up for the task. He encouraged me to apply for admission. So I did it, answered all the questions, with an essay that I really put my heart and soul into. You have to understand that this was one of those dreams I'd been holding for so very long. I had Blair write me a letter of recommendation. I applied and won acceptance. The major was decided for me, in a way: communications is what I am all about. My goal is to use all the life experiences, book smarts, and wisdom I can gather and speak to people—meet them where they are—to offer encouragement. Truly, I believe it's why God put me on this earth. To help others, to be His mouthpiece in a way.

I cannot say college life has been easy. I absolutely love my studies. But there are so many days when some ailment or another gets in the way. Days when the very best I can do is sit up in bed. It's very frustrating and disappointing. Because I registered for school with such high hopes. But here's what I know: I've got to just keep on keeping on.

That's the beauty of a life of service—to your family, husband, vocation, whatever it may be. When you know, and I mean really know in your bones like that "odd" bird, Jonathan Livingston Seagull—when you know your purpose, there's a clarity to the way you live your life.

I encourage all people, especially young people because we have moved so far away from the simple principles earlier generations were raised on: Get clear on your assignment. This world can twist you this way and that way. But if you are clear on your assignment, you won't—you can't—be led astray. I promise you, your duty will just flow from your heart.

Pearl of Duty

I encourage all people, especially young people, because we have moved so far away from the simple principles earlier generations were raised on: Get clear on your assignment. This world can twist you this way and that way. But if you are clear on your assignment, you won't—you can't—be led astray. I promise you, your duty will just flow from your heart.

Mom throwing the bouquet after her wedding, Buffalo, New York, 1960.

AFTERWORD

The nominations for theater's highest honors, the Tony Awards, were announced much later than usual due to the global pandemic. On October 15, 2020, it was one of the thrills of my life to be able to call Mom to tell her that her son was actually nominated for a Tony Award for Best Performance by an Actor in a Leading Role—in a Broadway production, no less. I played Captain Richard Davenport in *A Soldier's Play*. And, of course, the greatest source of inspiration for the role came from my family life and my relationship with my dad, a twenty-eight-year military veteran.

By this time, Mom was getting weaker and weaker with each passing day. In the old days, learning about such a huge career milestone, she would have squealed and hollered and called every person she knew—and some she didn't—to share the good news! But, unfortunately, she had been losing her will to live for quite some time. I would later learn that only weeks earlier, she had confided in a family friend that she was "tired and ready to go home" to her Lord.

AFTERWORD

When I called, via FaceTime, I could see that my father was lifting Mom out of bed and into her wheelchair. It was apparent that she was struggling and very likely in pain. I wanted to call back later, but my dad said that it was okay to talk now. When I gave them the news of the nomination, my dad was clearly preoccupied yet always supportive. He said, "Congratulations, son." But he remained laser focused on his wife and doing what he could to make her comfortable.

Understandably, there wasn't much of a reaction from either one of them. Mom settled into her chair, took a deep breath, and was barely able to utter the words: "That's great, Blair."

In that moment, I was struck by the cruel juxtaposition of worldly success—which is all an illusion—and the slipping away of the most vital life force I'd ever known: my mother. The same soul that breathed life into me was softly fading, not in despair but in quiet surrender.

I was beyond grateful to have been able to share that news with her. Even though she could not outwardly show her exuberance, I know the immense pride she felt inside. Because since the time I learned to walk I had seen her express her joy for every little accomplishment any one of her kids experienced. In fact, that was probably the first time I had ever encountered her unabashed expression of maternal joy, when I took my first steps. How ironic, that as I now observed my mother sitting in her wheelchair,

AFTERWORD

unable to walk, all I could think of was how profoundly proud of *her* I was and am. She bore her trials with quiet courage and never once complained. Even in the waning days of her life journey, she remained faithful, poised, elegant, composed, refined—and yes, the classic beauty.

Thirteen days later, in the early evening of October 28, 2020, my mother—the Marvelous Mrs. Marilyn Ann Underwood—was called Home to her Heavenly Father and gently rose into the arms of grace.

Mom at Coney Island, 1962.

ACKNOWLEDGMENTS

Foremost in my heart, I give thanks to my mother, the visionary who began this book fifty years ago. Though she did not live to see it completed, her words and spirit have guided me every step of the way. I owe her, well . . . everything. I must've been in the first grade when she first mentioned wanting to write a book. At the time, I didn't quite understand what she wanted to say in this book or why it was important to her. I later learned she inherently knew that her life was one of aspiration and a life well lived that would inspire and motivate others, if they would only pay attention. My parents taught me how to dream at a very young age and encouraged me to never cease dreaming until I took my last breath. That is exactly what she did. She carried with her a depth of soul, an understanding of God's will, and a vision for her future until her final breath. Even when her future was a glimpse into the realm beyond the veil, she dreamed.

ACKNOWLEDGMENTS

Even when it was time to step into God's eternal embrace with a perfected body no longer ravaged by the insidious nature of multiple sclerosis, still ... she dreamed. Then, finally, she crossed into the world of shining souls in which hers would shine ever so brightly. I consider it a blessing and the highest privilege to be her son and to bring her words forward, carrying her voice into the world.

To my extraordinary wife, Josie, my love for you knows no bounds. You embody so many of the qualities my mother possessed—self-assuredness, humility, class, beauty, loyalty, faithfulness, joy of spirit, boundless energy, and a limitless capacity to love. You knew my mother for over forty years and have often called her your mentor. I know she recognized so many of her virtues manifested in you and she longed to share her wisdom and insight as she witnessed you continue to shine throughout the years.

Dad, I am forever indebted to you for the man you are and at ninety-three years young, I am grateful for every moment we share together. You taught me how to be a man. You and Mom are undoubtedly my forever heroes! Together you raised us and built a foundation for my siblings and me that has bonded us in ways that can never be torn asunder. Though no marriage is perfect, yours was exemplary and you exhibited how to love your wife up to and including when she took her final breath. Absent in body but present in spirit, I looked through the

ACKNOWLEDGMENTS

fragile glass lens of my cell phone and witnessed how you held her hand in those final moments. I know and can "vouch-safe" your love for her until the very end.

To my siblings, Frank, Marlo, and Mellisa. We've shared so many unforgettable life experiences and memories with Mom and Dad. Thank you for walking this journey with me, for sharing our mother's heart, and for carrying her love. Her voice, spirit, and soul continue to guide us. She walks beside us, unseen but never absent. To my grandmother Bessie Scales, life was never easy but you gave me the greatest gift possible in giving birth to my mother. I was sixteen years old when you transitioned but I will never forget your spirit and laughter and, most of all, I will never forget the reverence my mother had for you. Without you, there is no Marilyn. I am overwhelmed with gratitude.

Ylonda Gault, I am eternally grateful. You took up the mantle of telling my mother's story and you have carried it across the finish line triumphantly. I could never thank you enough for bringing your considerable literary talents and using them to finally bring my mother's life story to fruition. She would, in her words, be "tickled pink" not only because you, too, are a Buffalo native but to see her memoir on bookshelves all over the world. Profound gratitude to the Buffalo History Museum and the hundreds of people you interviewed, including her circle of friends such as Timmye Fikes,

ACKNOWLEDGMENTS

Irene Prescott, Odell Reaves, Pamela Sussman, Dorothy Taylor, Veronica Dixon, and many more. All of which made sure every detail you sought to capture was contextual, accurate, and full of her loving spirit. You listened to countless hours of audio and video tapes, and in the end, you utterly captured her essence and voice. It is uncanny at times. Thank you for finishing the work my mom's hands begun so many years ago.

With deep appreciation that is difficult to put into words, I gratefully acknowledge my nine children and bonus children—Paris, Brielle, Blake, Summur, Randii, Brett, Blair, Brie, and Blakey. You are indeed our "life's work" and because being a parent is one of God's most cherished gifts, it gives me joy to be able to share the life and journey of the exceptional woman who raised me. If I am a successful parent in the least, it is due in great measure to the "blueprint" I had in her.

My heartfelt thanks and gratitude to Judith Curr. You continue to believe in me and support my abiding desire to touch people's lives in story form, whether fiction or nonfiction. Thank you sincerely for honoring my mother's life by seeing its value and helping it find its place in the world. This book would not and could not have seen the light of day without your imprimatur. Patrik Henry Bass, you have championed *A Soldier's Wife* from the very beginning. And for that I am forever grateful. These books never happen overnight. It takes patience,

ACKNOWLEDGMENTS

focus, dedication, drive, and passion. You have exhibited all of these virtues and more during this process. Thank you for keeping me on track with my deadlines and for your keen skill in crafting the story of my mother in literary form. You've done "yeoman's work" masterfully. Thank you Anayaé Holmes for all you've done in the completion of this memoir. Your emails and communications were always welcomed. Without you I don't think I would have been able to keep the trains running on time to finalize this process. Eric Suddleson, you always have my back and I am deeply grateful as I continue to traverse this "domain of imagination and ink," this world of literature. The legalities of this dance are often complicated but I am grateful to have you to translate and motivate me through it all. To Ron West, my longtime manager and friend. You've supported and encouraged me in all of my many endeavors. Publishing books and telling stories is an artistic muscle that I feel privileged to exercise. I can't thank you enough for continuing to believe in me and take the ride. Sydney Feyder, it doesn't happen without you, if you're not there to connect all the dots on a daily basis. I see you and I appreciate you and your attention to detail more than you know. Deborah Ainsworth, thank you for being so thorough and careful in all of my business dealings, especially in the construction of this "house of books" for the last twenty years. I deeply appreciate all that you have done and continue to

ACKNOWLEDGMENTS

do. Larry Roberts, you continue to guide and enlighten as this thing called "life" marches on. With profound gratitude to you sir, I tip my hat. I extend my heartfelt gratitude to Maria Rivera, whose loyal assistance and faithful presence have helped carry me through both the work and the life behind it. Finally, with a deep bow of gratitude, I offer thanks to all the mothers throughout time immemorial, whose instincts, love, and quiet strength have carried humanity forward. I am profoundly humbled to have been raised by one who is counted among the very best!

—Blair Underwood

ABOUT THE AUTHOR

Blair Underwood moves effortlessly across film, television, theater, and the literary world, shaping stories not only as an actor, but as a director, producer, and author.

In 2025, Underwood appeared in the feature film *Youngblood*, directed by Academy Award nominee Hubert Davis, which premiered at the Toronto International Film Festival, as well as the Netflix film *Don't Ever Wonder* with Nia Long and Larenz Tate.

In 2024, Underwood costarred with Nicolas Cage and Maika Monroe in the critically acclaimed thriller *Longlegs*, directed by Osgood Perkins. It broke box office records and became the highest-grossing opening for an original horror film that year. Additionally, he costarred in two series—the Starz drama *Three Women*, based on the bestselling novel; and the Sky TV UK romantic comedy *Smothered*. Earlier that year he also appeared in Ava DuVernay's heralded film *Origin*, an adaptation of

ABOUT THE AUTHOR

Isabel Wilkerson's bestselling book *Caste: The Origins of Our Discontents*.

Underwood recently directed, produced, and starred in the independent psychological thriller *Viral*, which is currently in post-production. *Viral* centers on Andrew (Underwood), who falls into a state of paranoia after his wife goes missing. The only way out of the self-destructive cycle seems to be through his new girlfriend Emilia (Sarah Silverman), who has her own psychological trauma to deal with.

Underwood secured his first Tony Award nomination as Best Lead Actor in a Play, having starred in the 2020 revival of the Pulitzer Prize–winning drama *A Soldier's Play* for director Kenny Leon and the Roundabout Theatre Company. The show received seven Tony nominations and won Best Revival of a Play. Underwood took his love for Broadway behind the scenes in 2021, serving as a producer of the new critically acclaimed show *Pass Over*, which was the first show to reopen Broadway after the COVID shutdown.

Past Netflix television credits include the Emmy Award–nominated limited series *Self Made: Inspired by the Life of Madam C. J. Walker* (for which he won an NAACP Image Award), Ava DuVernay's Emmy-winning limited series *When They See Us*, a recurring role on *Dear White People* and Clark Johnson's *Juanita*, opposite Alfre Woodard. He also appeared as Vernon Jordan in Ryan

ABOUT THE AUTHOR

Murphy's *Impeachment* for FX, HBO Max's *Love Life* and *Bad Hair* for Hulu. This season he also appeared as a murderous tennis coach in CBS's hit series *Elsbeth*. Underwood's series regular roles include the ABC drama series *Quantico* (which he filmed while also appearing in a recurring role on another hit ABC drama *Marvel's AGENTS OF S.H.I.E.L.D.*), *Dirty Sexy Money*, *The New Adventures of Old Christine*, *In Treatment*, *The Event*, and *L.A. Law*. Additional film credits include *Deep Impact*, *Set It Off*, *Rules of Engagement*, *Just Cause*, *Madea's Family Reunion*, and Steven Soderbergh's *Full Frontal*. Underwood costarred opposite Cicely Tyson in the Lifetime telefilm and theater production of *The Trip to Bountiful*, based on the Tony Award–winning play.

In 2012, he made his acclaimed Broadway debut in the iconic role of Stanley in Tennessee Williams's *A Streetcar Named Desire*, for which he earned a 2012 Drama League Distinguished Performance Award nomination. He also starred in *Paradise Blue* at the Williamstown Theatre Festival and *Othello* at the Old Globe Theatre.

He has also executive produced and narrated two critically acclaimed documentary features—Peabody Award–winning *Mr. SOUL!* and *Olympic Pride, American Prejudice*.

In 2009, he made his feature-film directing debut with *The Bridge to Nowhere*. He has also directed the 360-degree virtual reality Megadeth concert video

ABOUT THE AUTHOR

(for which he won a Clio Award), the short film *The Second Coming*, as well as several music videos and commercials.

Underwood is an Emmy Award winner (as producer of the philanthropy-centered Saturday morning series *Give*), a two-time Golden Globe Award nominee, and has been nominated for seventeen NAACP Image Awards (eight wins). He won a Grammy Award for Best Spoken Word as co-narrator of Al Gore's audiobook, *An Inconvenient Truth*. A member of the Academy of Motion Picture Arts and Sciences, he is also active in several philanthropic endeavors.